I GREW UP WITH BASKETBALL

I GREW UP WITH BASKETBALL

BASKETBALL

●

Twenty Years of Barnstorming with Cage Greats of Yesterday

BY FRANK J. BASLOE

In collaboration with
D. Gordon Rohman

Introduction by Michael A. Antonucci

UNIVERSITY OF NEBRASKA PRESS
LINCOLN AND LONDON

Introduction © 2012 by the Board of Regents of the University of
Nebraska

First Nebraska paperback printing: 2012

Library of Congress Cataloging-in-Publication Data
Basloe, Frank J., 1887–1966.
I grew up with basketball: twenty years of barnstorming with cage
greats of yesterday / Frank J. Basloe; in collaboration with D. Gordon
Rohman; introduction by Michael A. Antonucci.
p.   cm.
Originally published: New York: Greenberg, 1952.
Includes bibliographical references.
ISBN 978-0-8032-4023-0 (pbk.: alk. paper)
1. Basketball—History. I. Rohman, D. Gordon. II. Title.
GV885.B37 2012
796.323—dc23   2011045257

INTRODUCTION

Michael A. Antonucci

Legendary basketball promoter Frank J. Basloe delivers a deceptively simple account of his life and the sport's early years in *I Grew Up with Basketball*. As its title suggests, the memoir makes connections between basketball's inception and development and Basloe's career as a player and promoter, which he began at the age of sixteen. Presenting readers with an insider's perspective, *I Grew Up with Basketball* offers an eyewitness description of the many transformations basketball underwent during the years preceding the United States' entry into the First World War through the 1940s. Basloe's "life-in-sports" narrative covers the various changes in rules, equipment, and on-court strategies that basketball implemented during its formative years, including in-depth discussions of the game's promotional strategies and emerging professionalization.

At the same time, *I Grew Up with Basketball* also stands as an early twentieth-century coming-of-age tale. Accessing Basloe's childhood experiences as a Jewish Hungarian immigrant to the United States, the memoir reveals the writer's ambitions as well as the sense of possibility that he embraced in his adopted homeland. Central New York State and the Great Lakes region provide the backdrop for basketball's evolution and serve as Basloe's personal proving ground. The game's progression from an amateur, indoor, recreational activity to a highly competitive professional team sport, with a passionate and devoted fan base, comes to reflect the writer's personal Americanization process.

Throughout the course of *I Grew Up with Basketball*, Basloe conducts a guided tour of basketball's foundations, recognizing its dimensions as a sport and an industry. Observers of contemporary men's basketball as it is played at both the professional and elite collegiate level in the early twenty-first century will immediately recognize situations that Basloe describes: questionable officiating, star players and money, management's financial concerns, grueling travel schedules, and fan belligerence—to the point of violence—are all described in the text.

Topics emerging from this narrative are as familiar as any given day's sports news cycle. For instance, Basloe's maxim that "championships are bought and paid for" is as relevant today as it was for the barnstorming squads he proclaimed as "World Champions." *I Grew Up with Basketball* also brings attention to a series of unexpected sites marking the game's early history, including general stores and YMCAs in upstate New York; armories and auditoriums from Albany to Fond du Lac, Wisconsin; a long line of whistle-stop hotels and the New York Central Rail Road; and freight yards in Ft. Wayne, Indiana, where angry workers were striking.

I Grew Up with Basketball exceeds conventional expectations of a "sports history" volume. Recounting his contributions to basketball's popularity as a pioneering player and promoter, Basloe chronicles the sport's transformative capacities by recalling his movement from a "greenhorn" to a "high-toned American." The narrative reflects upon a range of subjects that intersect in conversations concerning nation, sport, and identity; third-wave immigration to the United States, ethnicity, and whiteness illustrate the way sports—particularly basketball—provide individuals and groups with an identity source while they confront rapidly changing social and cultural landscapes. Through his firsthand account of the ways in which the game of basketball captured the imaginations of athletes and audiences across the United States, Basloe offers a provocative set of insights into how sports and entertainment intersected in the early twentieth century in small towns and industrial urban settings.

My first encounter with Frank J. Basloe's *I Grew Up with Basketball* took place while I was developing a first-year writing course at the University of Illinois–Chicago. I was interested in having students explore basketball and write about the game as a feature on the social and cultural landscape of the United States. During the opening years of the twenty-first century, UIC was clearly the right place for developing this type of course. Although the 1998 NBA lockout and Michael Jordan's (second) retirement clearly had marked the end of an era in the game's history, daydreams about Jordan's (first) comeback and the Bulls' second three-peat championship run persisted among UIC students. The Bulls—*those* Bulls, the ones with Scottie Pippen and Phil Jackson, Dennis Rodman and Michael Jordan—had made a profound imprint on the generation of Chicagoans entering college at the outset of what was referred to as the "new millennium." Like other youths across the United States (or, for that matter, around the globe), these students had been instructed "to be like Mike" for as long as they could remember; over the course of their Clinton-era free-market childhoods, their choices in sports drinks, processed snack foods, or sports footwear were shaped by Jordan's invisible hand. In addition to leading the local hardwood pros to the promised land on the court, off the court Jordan (aka "Jumpman," aka "Flight Lesson") showed his teammates ways of achieving new levels of dedifferentiated sports marketing. As 'ballers and pitch-men, they learned to hit their targets hard. In this respect Jordan and the Bulls would have made barnstorming Frank Basloe and his Globe Trotters very proud.

On the afternoon that I found a copy of *I Grew Up with Basketball* in the stacks of the Richard J. Daley Library, I could not have imagined that a memoir recalling basketball as it was played in the first half of the twentieth century would be readily accessible to my students. I hoped that, at best, a few selected chapters from this yellowed volume would provide a backdrop for class discussions about the game's history. I was looking to contextualize aspects of the game *older* than the Magic-Bird/Lakers-Celtics rivalry of the 1980s or to extend our conversation about the game's relationship to fans to *before* the rise of the TNT cable network. I'd come to see that the values of professional basketball in the Dream Team–era NBA—particularly the relentless promotion of star players—had eclipsed the game's humble origins to a point where the conditions had become nearly unimaginable. (For instance, CBS actually did broadcast NBA playoff games on tape delay, including games two and five of the 1980 NBA Finals!) I hoped that Basloe's narrative might successfully edge our classroom discussions beyond the limits established in the NBA's recent history of financial and marketing successes.

Ultimately, *I Grew Up with Basketball* was able to help students reconsider numerous assumptions and associations that situated basketball and basketball players—both on and off the court—as fixed points within contemporary conversations about urban environments and African American identity in the United States. At the time that I pulled the text from its library shelf, the Mahmoud Abdul-Rauf "Star-Spangled Banner" controversy and Latrell Spreewell's assault on P. J. Carlisimo were significant milestones in the minds

of American sports fans, measuring a growing distance between African American athletes and their predominantly
white audiences and management teams. At the same time,
the NBA itself was undergoing a set of monumental transi-
tions, both in Chicago and throughout the world. As Jordan's comeback as a Washington Wizard came and went,
Kobe Bryant was being investigated in Colorado for sex-
ual assault, and Commissioner David Stern issued a dress-
code decree and intervention against hip-hop style, the sport
found itself in the midst of another moment of "before/af-
ter" transformation. With Basloe's narrative, it is possible to
make a case that basketball has existed in a perpetual state
of transition, not unlike the condition of "a changing same"
that poet Amiri Baraka ascribes to African American music.

I was pleasantly surprised by my students' response to the
Basloe narrative. Their engagement with the text seemed
to follow two patterns. A few of the individuals who found
their way to my classroom were confirmed Chicago sports
fans, complete with full-color memories of games and plays
executed by Jordan and the Bulls. Nearly all of the students,
however, were able to recall marketable items that promoted
the team or its players, including the soft fun of the Tony Ku-
koc beanbag toy, the seemingly endless possibilities invested
in the Dennis Rodman action figure (complete with pierc-
ings, tattoos, and "interchangeable heads"), or the taste of
McDonald's Beef Wennington sandwich (named in honor
of Bulls big man Bill Wennington). Most of the participants
in the course were first-generation college students; impor-
tantly, many of these students were either first-generation
Americans or themselves immigrants. Students with these
experiences brought an interesting set of perspectives to the
Basloe narrative that redirected our conversations about basketball, moving the focus away from the familiar talk of are-
nas, scoreboards, statistics, and standings. When read as an

immigrant success tale, *I Grew Up with Basketball* offers a chronicle of Basloe's desire to distinguish himself within particularly American contexts. It thereby spans the distance separating Basloe and his early twentieth-century basketball teams from an audience of college students consisting primarily of emerging adults in early twenty-first-century Chicago.

Basloe's memoir also complements scholarly examinations of basketball's emergence as both a sport and social phenomena in the early twentieth-century United States. The insider's perspective in *I Grew Up with Basketball* speaks to historical studies of the sport such as Robert W. Peterson's *Cages to Jump Shots: Pro Basketball's Early Years*. Like Basloe, Peterson delivers an account of the game's early years that recognizes that the rough-and-tumble manner of play on the court was matched by a volatile movement of players, rules, leagues, and affiliations. While Peterson pointedly casts doubt on Basloe's claims identifying Herkimer, New York, as both the incubator for amateur basketball *and* a significant point of genesis for the professional game, his study contextualizes Basloe's accounts of his travels through New York State and the Great Lakes region, locating his Globe Trotters among other early basketball barnstormers.

Cages and *I Grew Up with Basketball* both acknowledge the American sporting public's attraction to basketball. According to Peterson, an interested public, willing to pay to see basketball played by professionals, gave rise to barnstorming teams such as the New York Wanderers as well as numerous regional professional leagues. He writes that "by the late 1890s there were scores of professional teams in the Philadelphia–New York area, southern New England, the Hudson River Valley of New York State, and eastern and southeastern Pennsylvania."[1] A symbiotic relationship between the traveling teams and local squads developed, effectively helping to promote the sport's popularity. Citing the memoir of pioneering basketballer Marvin A. Riley, Peterson supports Basloe's claims of the various opportunities basketball posed for enterprising, young sportsmen as a new century began in the United States. Peterson quotes Riley's statement that he set an earnings record for a single basketball game in the 1901–2 season by refereeing for 10 percent of the gate receipts on a night when the box office grossed $1,200.[2] Sixteen-year-old Frank Basloe's impulse was to begin his career as a basketball promoter by printing sheets of "Herkimer Team—Champions of the Mohawk Valley" letterhead to book a string of games for his team in New York's north country during the winter of 1903.

I Grew Up with Basketball also resonates with Murry R. Nelson's "Basketball as Cultural Capital: The Original Celtics in Early Twentieth-Century New York City." Drawing upon Pierre Bordieu's "cultural capital" concept, Nelson argues that sports facilitate individual and collective integration into mainstream American culture. To advance this position he states, very plainly, that "basketball became cultural capital for many New York City immigrants in the early 1900s."[3] Discussing cultural capital as a sort of "screen and filter," Nelson draws upon the experiences of the Original Celtics to explore immigration, loyalty, and the construction of ethnic identity in the United States. He notes that this legendary New York–based barnstorming basketball team originated as a settlement house team from Chelsea, which at the time had a reputation as a tough, Irish, working-class district. While making the case that "basketball served as cultural capital for a number of immigrant groups, particularly the Irish, the Germans, and the Jews," Nelson suggests that the sport provided members of these ethnic groups with "an investment in both American culture and a modified re-investment in these immigrant cultures."[4]

Basloe's narrative heartily supports Nelson's assertion, verifying that participation among ethnic groups—both as spectators and players—made a significant impact on the game. *I Grew Up with Basketball* provides an illustration of this dynamic through Basloe's accounts of games that his teams played against the Buffalo Germans and the Ogdensburg "fighting Irish," among other ethnically identified squads. Over the course of his memoir, Basloe also recalls entering the cage personally to play with and against players from a variety of backgrounds. He recounts taking the court with Jewish American players, like himself, as well as with "Swede" Grimstead and Jim Murnane, whom he describes as "a real Mohawk Dutchman." Basloe also recalls playing with and against Irish Americans, German Americans, Native Americans, and African Americans.

Significantly, Basloe also demonstrates a keen awareness of the powerful use (as well as the misuse) of racial and ethnic markers as promotional devices in sports. Basloe provides an extended description of the ruse that he and his players enacted on the Metropolitan Five of New York City during back-to-back games in Oswego. He writes:

In those days I had my stationery printed with "Oswego Indians" at the top. Swede Grimstead, a pal of these New York lads, wrote them about the "Indians." [They] wrote back to ask if Swede was playing with "real" Indians. Swede got a big laugh out of the letter and showed it around. . . . [A]rdent Oswego fans . . . saw a chance to have some fun with the city slickers. So they formed a "tribe," along with Johnny White, the druggist at Hennesey's, and Swede. . . . Over at the Armory, Shorty and Jacky White were setting the scene, painting the faces of the Oswego team to look like Indians, mine included. (93)

Ultimately, the sort of red-face minstrelsy practiced by Basloe's Oswego Indians proved to be an interesting precursor to a game that his 1915 barnstorming squad played in Odannah, Wisconsin, against a team of Native American cagers. In his description of the event, Basloe writes, "When we arrived, I was told how to get to the reservation. Imagine our astonishment when we found that the manager was a real Wild West Indian chief with beautiful black hair and scanty beard" (153).

In moments such as this, *I Grew Up with Basketball* lends support to Nelson's claim that basketball functions as a means of advancement for both individuals and groups. He suggests that the process of cultural capital accumulation occurs on multiple levels, writing, "The challenge for members of the non-dominant classes is to determine what appropriate cultural capital is and how to acceptably obtain it since how one acquires such capital is as important as the acquisition itself."[5] Both Nelson and Basloe identify this phenomenon as an outgrowth of basketball's unique development pattern. Basloe identifies the game as "an unruly bear cub in the family of sports." Similarly, Nelson maintains that basketball "moved from amateur game to professional spectator sport" by following a distinct path. Citing Bourdieu's sociological examinations of popular sports,[6] Nelson explains that these developments were fostered "in educational establishments reserved for . . . bourgeois society." "Professional basketball was produced by the people," he continues, and it "returned to the people in the form of spectacles produced for the people . . . as one branch among others of show business."[7] Nelson's essay establishes an appropriate framework for contextualizing and exploring basketball's early years as they are depicted in *I Grew Up with Basketball.*

At certain points, Basloe's narrative reads like an extended listing of unfamiliar names wrapped around a detailed account of games won and lost long ago. Yet even in those moments when *I Grew Up with Basketball* takes the form of

an annals, it succeeds in spite of itself. Careful readers will
find themselves coming into direct contact with a number
of early basketball's most recognizable figures, including
Hall of Famers such as the Minneapolis Lakers' gentle giant George Mikan, members of the Original Celtics, and the
Harlem Globetrotters' promoter and founder, Abe Saperstein. Among the many names Basloe casually drops in the
course of his memoir is that of Chuck Taylor, designer of
the iconic high-top basketball shoe. Taylor makes the list by
virtue of playing for Basloe during the 1919–20 season; he
is described as "a big, rangy kid" with the "stamp of hunger
. . . bitten deep into [his] face." Basloe writes that "he never
looked rested or well fed" but that he "saw that Chuck Taylor was a great star" (188–89).

Packed with references and anecdotes such as these, *I
Grew Up with Basketball* deserves the attention of scholars
and students across a range of academic fields. The perspective it brings to basketball's development on the court,
as well as its place within American popular culture and as
a business, presents a significant challenge to the way that
both general audiences and academic readers conceive of
basketball history. As much as the image of Dr. James Naismith hanging peach baskets in the gymnasium of a YMCA
in Springfield, Massachusetts, persists in the game's genesis
tale, *I Grew Up with Basketball* complicates this narrative and
its dependence on a single site and single creator. Despite
Basloe's attempts to revise the game's origin myth through
substitution (Herkimer, New York, for Springfield, Massachusetts; Lambert Will for Naismith; heads of cabbage for
the now legendary peach baskets), his memoir effectively
reminds readers that sports innovations are cultural innovations, produced through the process of collaboration and
experiment, carried out over time and in multiple spaces.

When read in this way, *I Grew Up with Basketball* addresses concerns novelist and cager John Edgar Wideman raises in "Who Invented the Jump Shot (A Fable)." In this fantastic essay-meets-meta-fiction experiment, Wideman interrogates the processes by which history is made. With his narrator moving freely through dimensions of time and space, Wideman's readers are placed inside a Studebaker sedan driven by Abe Saperstein on a particularly cold evening in January 1927. In this way Wideman brings readers to the legendary basketball promoter as he is carrying members of the original Harlem Globetrotters from Chicago to Hinckley, Illinois, for their inaugural game. Straddling the line between historical fiction and creative nonfiction, Wideman's act of literary imagination stands as his response to an overflow audience attending a panel session titled "Who Invented the Jump Shot" at a meeting of the Association for the Study of Popular Culture.

At the outset of this meditation on myth, fiction, history, and possibility, Wideman writes, "The title of the session let the cat out of the bag. It broadcast two faulty assumptions—that at some particular moment the jump shot appeared, new and fully formed as Athena popping from the head of Zeus, and that a single individual deserved credit for originating the jump shot."[8] Distrusting the process by which folk culture and the collaborative practice become codified and commodified, Wideman's narrator suggests: "'Who Invented the Jump Shot' would be a pissing contest. And guess who will win. Not my perpetually outnumbered, outvoted, outgunned side. Huh-uh. No way. My colleagues of the Euro persuasion will claim one of their own, a white college kid on such and such a night in such and such an obscure area proved by such and such musty dusty documents, launched the first jump shot. It would be a coming out party for the scholar who invents the inventor."[9] Before summoning a literary vision of Abe Sapperstein's Studebaker in the winter of 1927, Wideman's narrator assesses the panel when he flatly states, "By the end of two hours they'll own the jump shot, unimpeachable experts on its birth, development and death. Rewriting history, planting their flag on a chunk of territory because nobody's around to holler *Stop thief.*"[10]

Basloe's *I Grew Up with Basketball* also collects for its readers a set of questions about the game's legacy and image. Firstly, the memoir's age and cultural distance from today's readers almost necessarily require that they ask how it maintains its relevance to conversations about basketball at the outset of the twenty-first century's second decade. Similarly, it's important to inquire if particular patterns and styles demonstrated by Basloe's prewar barnstorming squads maintain tangible connections to players, teams, and prospects present in contemporary basketball. These inquires may be followed up by asking how Basloe's narrative impacts the work of researchers and writers interested in locating and identifying the white ethnic past of a sport that is widely regarded as a nearly exclusive domain of African American athletes. What does *I Grew Up with Basketball* suggest to readers invested in this project? How does it complicate their notions of the game and its origins? The astounding amount of information about basketball's early years that is divulged in Basloe's narrative seems to push the question: does this information reorganize our thinking about the game's development and structure?

Although the impulse is commonplace, perhaps even cliched, questions concerning the relevance of *I Grew Up with Basketball* to the game in the twenty-first century almost inevitably reference the figure of LeBron James. Many aspects of King James's career maintain a resonance with the basic premise Basloe follows in the course of his narrative: basketball can be a profitable enterprise for a young person with the proper desire and ambition. This idea becomes clear early in the book when Basloe returns to Herkimer after his initial barnstorming trip to New York State's north country: "[I] tramped home, [and] there was Papa at the front gate with a broom handle, ready to give me the beating of my life. . . . I pulled out my $300 and waved it in front of him. That was more than he had made in a whole year at Diemel and Snell's Lumber Yard. Or at the store in two months. I had earned it in a week!" (51–52).

Similarly, along with the crush of media attention and public expectations that defined the opening phase of LeBron James's basketball career—that is, his visibility in high school playing with the Fighting Irish of St. Vincent–St. Mary's in Akron to his emergence as a perennial NBA All-Star—King James became synonymous with the acquisition of numerous, lucrative playing and endorsement contracts. Not surprisingly, the second phase of his career, which corresponds with the frustrating runs his Cleveland Cavaliers made into the NBA playoffs—including an unsuccessful trip to the Finals in 2007—is also associated with off-court promotional posturing activity that might have made even Frank J. Basloe blush. Between the much-discussed and highly criticized ESPN-produced television spectacle known as "The Decision"—where James announced his intention to end his free agency by signing a six-year $110.1 million contract with the Miami Heat—and the photo-op/pep rally held with his new teammates Dwyane Wade and Chris Bosh, the King has worked in the razzle dazzle footprints of Basloe's Globe Trotters and those who followed, taking these old dances to unprecedented levels.

Beyond the hype and commentary that has surrounded James and his free-agent signing with Miami, basketball fans, writers, and commentators from numerous quarters have witnessed the unfolding of messy revelations and accusations surrounding NBA officials and gambling. This betting scandal, which led to the conviction and imprisonment of former NBA official Tim Donaghy on conspiracy to commit wire fraud and other charges, provides a platform for examining questions about the role that referees and gambling play in the game. *I Grew Up with Basketball* poignantly reminds readers that the Donaghy scandal and accusations that have emerged in its wake are not exactly news bulletins to basketball insiders. In the course of his memoir, Basloe repeatedly questions the objectivity of referees. His lighthearted critiques of game officials seem to suggest that their local bias was an expected part of "home field" advantage. For example, in the description he gives of a game his barnstormers played in Bismarck, North Dakota, Basloe recalls how the game was preceded by a foul-shooting contest between the two teams. He writes, "At last the game began. The referee was a local man and, of course, he wanted to be very fair. After seeing [our player's poor] foul shooting, he was sure he could call unlimited fouls against the home team and not hurt their chances. So he called 15 on them. But [our player] fooled him. He made 14 of those 15 shots, much to the dismay of the Bismarck players" (150).

This contest was part of a western swing that Basloe made during the 1914–15 season with the Cornstarch Quintet, a team that he considered among the best he ever assembled. Earlier on the trip, this squad of players was harassed on and off the court by a group of Chicago gangsters who had booked a series of games between Basloe's team and the Mercury Athletic Club. Despite the presence of Chicago mayor "Big Bill" Thompson and other prominent political figures, a haze of impropriety hung over the first of these games, which was played on a court on the fourth floor of a low-rise building on the city's West Side.[11] Following this contest Basloe and his players required assistance from police to make it to their hotel.

Given these and other intersections that *I Grew Up with Basketball* has with conversations surrounding the contemporary game—both professional and collegiate—it would appear that Basloe's memoir has found a suitable time to return to print. Several distinct similarities emerge when considering early basketball and today's game, but none is perhaps greater than the way that the game—seemingly more so than any other predominant North American team sport—is defined and shaped by the excitement created as it is played in the moment. There's a deep and decided gap separating today's heroes and yesterday's legends. If you want to test this idea, ask someone under the age of twenty-five about Allen Iverson, Patrick Ewing, Karl Malone, or Reggie Miller. Even in the age of digital video archives, it is unlikely that he or she will be able to recall just how good these players were.

I Grew Up with Basketball works against the totalizing historical impulses that Wideman describes in "Who Invented the Jumpshot." Rather than the neatly organized and clearly delineated genealogy of development that the fable's panel of (so-called) experts would like to establish, Basloe's narrative delivers a diverse set of perspectives that trace the development of the sport. Through the ambiguity of its homespun, personalized accounts, *I Grew Up with Basketball* fashions a crazy quilt of experience, from the events of long-forgotten games (the 31st Separate Company of Herkimer's 38–31 victory over the North Adam Stars in 1906) to faded names of heroes (Ed Wachter, Jim Davy, and Ed Doran) and accounts of unlikely roundball powerhouses (the Brattleboro Athletics and Co. D of St. Johnsbury). Basloe's memoir responds to Wideman's concerns about the production of sports history and at the same time addresses those questions presented by Pierre Bordieu, Murry R. Nelson, LeBron James, and anyone else who has dribbled and run on hardwood.

Notes

1. Robert W. Peterson, *Cages to Jump Shots: Pro Basketball's Early Years* (New York: Oxford University Press, 1990), 39.

2. Compare his $120 cut to the $769 average household income in the United States for 1901. U.S. Bureau of Labor Statistics, *100 Years of U.S. Consumer Spending: Data for the Nation, New York City, and Boston* (2006), www.bls.gov/opub/uscs/1901.pdf.

3. Murry R. Nelson, "Basketball as Cultural Capital: The Original Celtics in Early Twentieth-Century New York City," *Immigrants and Minorities* 17, no. 1 (1998): 69.

4. Nelson, "Basketball as Cultural Capital," 82.

5. Nelson, "Basketball as Cultural Capital," 69.

6. See Pierre Bourdieu, "How Can One Be a Sports Fan?" in *The Cultural Studies Reader*, ed. S. During (London: Routledge, 1993), 339–55.

7. Nelson, "Basketball as Cultural Capital," 69.

8. John Edgar Wideman, "Who Invented the Jump Shot (A Fable)," in *Hoop Roots* (Boston: Houghton Mifflin, 2001), 137.

9. Wideman, "Who Invented the Jump Shot," 137.

10. Wideman, "Who Invented the Jump Shot," 137.

11. The site is located just blocks away from the Richard J. Daley Library and University of Illinois–Chicago campus.

Gratefully Dedicated to

Lawrence Skiddy,

one of the game's pioneers and a perennial champion of the youthful player and the underdog. It was he, more than anyone else, who inspired me with the confidence I needed to write this book,

and to

All the great players on all my teams,
without whom I could have achieved nothing.

CONTENTS

PREFACE

THIS IS A BOOK about basketball first. Secondly it is a book about the town of Herkimer's claim to basketball fame. Thirdly it is a book about how I grew up with basketball.

In this book you will read either again or for the first time about the stars of old, about the big men and little men who made basketball into the splendid game it is today.

In this book you will read how James Naismith invented the game of basketball in Springfield, Mass. How he sent suggestions to different YMCA's around the East. How the physical director of the Herkimer Y, Lambert Will, took these suggestions and made a game of them. How the first basketball game was played in the Herkimer Y. How later the first professional game was played in Herkimer.

In this book you will read how I became a basketball promoter at sixteen. How stars like Lew Wachter, Jim Murnane, Mike Roberts, Jimmy Williamson, Bradley Hall, Jim Conway, Jack Andre, Jack Nolls, the Bradshaw twins, Oscar Grimstead, "Toots" McBride, Shan Kellmurray, Bill Dowd, Bill Ladeseaur, Bobby Hammond, "Blubs" Alberding, Leo Duval, Al Schuler, Ed Kearney, "Jerk" Waters played on my teams. You will read how my team in 1910 stopped the great winning streak of the Buffalo Germans after the Germans had won 110 straight. How two years later another of my teams defeated the Germans three out of four games and became "World Champions."

In this book you will read how the Oswego Giants, better known as the Basloe Globe Trotters, went on a tour through the Midwest spreading the gospel of basketball. You will discover the enthusiasm that greeted this tour, how whole towns turned out to greet the team at the station with bands and torch light parades. You will read of halls overflowing with people, of local gamblers making all sorts of impossible wagers on the home team, of the sale of "World Championship Banners," of riots and fights over the games, of parties and personages, travel and hardships on the road in pre-World War I America. In all, the Basloe Globe Trotters traveled better than 94,000 miles.

I have seen an immense number of basketball games in fifty years. Basketball and I grew up together. Basketball gave me my education. I left grade school to manage it. I learned about business and about people from basketball.

I learned about gifted young men like Ed Wachter, Barney Sedran, Lawrence Skiddy, Dick Leary, Johnny Stark, Jack Inglis, Bill Hardman, Sandy Shields, Simp Peterson, George Young, Ziggy Thompson, George Fogarty, Joe Fogarty, Toby Mathews, Chuck Soladare, Bill Johnson, Elmer Ripley, Paddy Driscoll, Fritz Chrisler, Trim McInstry, Harry Hough, Bob Hasbrook, Homer Stonebreaker, Johnny Beckman, Pete Barry, Marty Barry, Don Risley, Alan Gould, Al Heerdt, Bert Post, "Chief" Muller, Ed Garrity, Bill Schardt, Elmer Bloom, Bill Reed, Oscar Koult and more. Growing up with them was an education.

Basketball today is not basketball of fifty years ago. But basketball today is no superior to the game of fifty years ago. The great passing, speed and defensive play of my time are all too little in evidence on courts today. This book will show you the difference in the two styles of play.

This book will first take you into a little general store in Herkimer at Christmas time, 1890. It will show you Lambert Will putting an idea to work and giving Herkimer and the world its first basketball game. It will show you the growth of basketball, the spread of its fever. It will show you how I came to America and started growing with the sport. From then on, my story and the story of basketball are the same.

In writing this book I have had the help of many kind people. Records, clippings, pictures, and letters have been sought from all parts of the country. First I would like to thank Edward Beckingham of Herkimer, whose sixty-year-old scrapbook produced articles in newspapers which proved that basketball was played in Herkimer in 1891. Then there is the grand old man of basketball, Lambert Will, now living at Nelson, New York, just outside of Syracuse. Others are Charles Wright of Fond du Lac, Wisconsin, for his efforts in supplying the history of basketball in his state; Fred Cooper for his valuable newspaper clippings showing the part Trenton, New Jersey, had in shaping basketball; Roy Fairman of the *Syracuse Herald Journal* for a great deal of basketball history; Bill Scheffer of the *Philadelphia Inquirer* for the early history of basketball in Pennsylvania; C. E. Broughton, editor of the *Sheboygan Press*, Sheboygan, Wisconsin, for the early history of basketball in Wisconsin; Paul Williams, editor of the *Utica Daily Press*, for his publicity and fine co-operation during our trips out West; Cornelia Taylor Fairbanks, librarian at the St. Johnsbury (Vermont) Library, for the early history of basketball in St. Johnsbury; Bob Dubuque, Sports Editor of *The Reformer*, Brattleboro, Vermont, for his early history of basketball in the state of Vermont; Charlotte Bloom, Rochester, New York, for valuable information; Len Wilbur, Sports Editor of the *Utica Daily Press and Observer;* Honorable Judge Carl Peterson, Surrogate of Herkimer Co.; Mary B. Myers and Rosemarie Paestello, my secretaries; and last but not least the members of my family, Irving and Ann Basloe, Jerry and Eleanor Levin, Sheldon and Norma Basloe, and Arthur and Leatrice Golden.

So on to my story. As Charles E. Wilson, former head of General Electric, put it in a letter to me not long ago, "basketball in days past was pretty bush league. We didn't make much money, but we had a lot of fun trying just the same."

THE AUTHOR

I GREW UP WITH BASKETBALL

CHAPTER ONE

THEY STARTED WITH
CABBAGES

I WAS THREE the Christmas that Lambert Will hustled into Ausman's General Store. The year was 1890. There were only 2700 people in my home town of Herkimer, N. Y., that year. Most of the folks in our little village lived in frame houses clustered along elm-lined streets next to the main tracks of the New York Central Railroad where it split the Mohawk Valley.

Lambert Will had a pamphlet in his pocket when he entered the store, shaking powder snow from his coat. It was 20 degrees below zero.

Old Emery Ausman, proprietor, was out in that cold helping to bury a man. Some out-of-towners had found a corpse sprawled among a lot of kindling wood. It was a mighty cold day to bury a man.

After a hearty exchange of season's greetings, Lambert took off his coat and joined the crowd of town planters around the coal-fired oak stove. There was a pitch game in progress. The stove was spattered yellow-brown with tobacco juice.

Piled in tempting displays throughout the store were fine Herkimer County cheeses, home-cured hams, crates of walnuts and butternuts, barrels of pungent apple cider, bushel baskets chuck full of potatoes, carrots, beets, squash, onions, and cabbages hard as bullets.

Under the glass case on the counter were trays of ribbon candy and hard candy, molasses taffy, peanut brittle, dried fruits of all kinds, and fresh-smelling doughnuts. Back on the shelves behind the counter lay countless spools of silk thread, mysterious bottles of Lydia Pinkham's Compound, Father John's medicine, packages of snuff, and Warnecke and Brown's tobacco. The place smelled good.

Big Simp Peterson was behind the counter waiting on the just-before-Christmas shoppers come to purchase a shirt, ax, cheese, or spool of thread. Simp was the strongest boy in the village. Another young lad, Fritz Gray, was lounging about the card players.

Will motioned to Simp and Fritz to join him on a bench in the rear of the store. Simp sauntered over and Fritz followed.

Everyone in town knew Lambert Will. It was just a month since he had become physical director of Herkimer's brand new YMCA. Because the Y didn't have much money, Will had volunteered his services.

This day he was burning with an idea. The pamphlet he was carrying in his pocket had started him thinking.

"Got somethin' to show you boys," he said. He tugged a piece of paper from his coat. "Look here. It tells about a new game somebody down East thought of."

Simp and Fritz Gray sat down beside Will.

"In this game—he calls it 'basketball'—you try to throw a ball into a peach basket. Least that's what Naismith used. He's the guy wrote this." Will indicated the pamphlet with his finger.

Dr. James Naismith, too, was a Y physical education director. And he had had a problem. When cold weather forced his students indoors at the Springfield (Massachusetts) YMCA, he discovered the dull gymnastic routines of the day didn't hold their interest. So young Jim Naismith devised a new game.

Naismith mentally developed his new game, typed up some "letters," and sent them around to other YMCA's in the country. One of these letters came to Lambert Will.

"Don't sound like much to me," put in Simp Peterson.

"Yeah, what's the object?" chorused Fritz.

Will leaned toward the two. "You boys know we need some sort of game to play at the Y. This is it. You don't need many men. You don't need much room. And you can play it inside, in the winter. Stead of holing up in Em's store like you do."

"But peach baskets . . ." Simp started.

Will was not to be denied. "Look, you put nine men on a side. Nail the peach baskets on a wall twelve feet up or so, one at each end of the room. Then, according to this letter, the teams roll the ball back and forth. One team tries to take it away from the other. The team with the ball gets it down to one end near a basket and tosses it up. If it goes in, they score a point."

The boys didn't look convinced.

The door opened. Old Em Ausman came in with a draft of cold air which disturbed the pitch players huddled around the glowing stove. He stomped the snow off his boots and roared, "Hey, Simp, got any cider on the floor?"

"Nope. Barrel's empty."

"Well, fetch up some more then," he ordered.

Simp marched off to the cellar, cradled a barrel of applejack in his brawny arms, and carried it upstairs. Em Ausman looked on with satisfaction.

"Now then," he said, helping himself to a generous glassful, "what's with you boys?"

"Simp," said Lambert Will, "do you think old Em here would let us try out this game in the store?"

Irked at not being asked directly—for he was a good-hearted man—Em stopped the question dead with a "Boys, try anything. Just don't break the kerosene lamps."

"Got any peach baskets?" asked Will.

"Yes, but you can't use them. They're full of walnuts and butternuts. Dump out some of those potatoes over there and use bushel baskets. Say, what you need baskets for anyway?"

But the boys were off preparing the field for action. Simp and Will grabbed two of Em's seven-foot stepladders and put the emptied baskets on top of them. Will directed the placing of the ladders. Fritz shoved aside some of the produce that lay in scattered heaps around the floor. The pitch players stared in silence at the preparations. You couldn't play pitch with all that commotion.

"What are we going to use for a medicine ball?" asked Fritz.

That one almost stumped Will. That is, until he spied the piles of cabbages near the counter.

"Here's just the thing. We'll use cabbages for balls." Then he turned. "Of course, it it's all right with Em . . ."

"Yah, go ahead. Nobody's buying cabbages for Christmas anyway. What you going to do, throw them into the basket?"

"That's the idea," Will said.

Old Em scratched his head. This was something new. It might be foolish. But darned if he wasn't one to go along with a joke. "Say, you fellows, if that's what you're going to do, I'll tell you what I'm going to do. I'll give the boy that puts the most cabbages in the baskets a glass of cider and a doughnut." He kicked the barrel that Simp had just lugged up.

All activity in the store centered around the exhibition of cabbage throwing. Outside the kerosene street lights were on and horse cars were delivering workers from Ilion. Shoppers joined the gallery of spectators around the stove to watch the strange contest.

"Each boy gets ten shots apiece," decided Will. Simp went over to the pile of home-grown cabbages, selected a large, firm head and took his place about twelve feet in front of the stepladder with the potato basket on top. He began to toss the vegetable up in the air, dangerously close to the hanging lamps and into the basket. Out of ten tries, he made six "baskets."

Then Fritz Gray stepped up and began throwing. He, too, made six "baskets."

Lambert Will then took his turn with the same head of cabbage. Up and in, up and in, the head sailed. The spectators "oh'ed" and "ah'ed" with each throw. More joined the circle of the curious when the people outside began to realize that something was going on inside Ausman's store. It didn't hurt Em's business, all this attention.

Lambert ended with the same total as the others, six baskets. So it was up to Em to dole out the promised cider and eats, which he did generously. Everyone else wanted to try his hand at the game. But Em had had enough for one day. The head of cabbage did not look the worse for wear. But even home-grown Herkimer cabbage was not indestructible. And those throws were coming dangerously close to the swaying lamps. Em was satisfied. He gave the cider and doughnuts as much for the fact that the lamps were still intact as for rewarding athletic ability.

The crowd broke up. People hurried home for supper. Many had gifts to buy for the holiday. Others were going to fetch hatchets. They would be off to the hills to chop down a Christmas tree. For a time they forgot about "basketball."

But Lambert Will didn't. The game intrigued him. There were so many possibilities! There were so many details yet to work out before it could be called a "game." Cabbages were poor substitutes for balls. So while other good citizens of Herkimer went off to enjoy the Yuletide, Lambert set himself to the task of working up "basketball" into something that could be played.

CHAPTER TWO

THE WORLD'S FIRST
BASKETBALL GAME

IT WAS after that Christmas of 1890 that the boys got together for a real practice session at the YMCA. Lambert Will, Simp Peterson, and Fritz Gray had passed the
word around town. Eighteen boys showed up on the appointed day.

Will decided that, as in baseball, there should be nine
men to a team. He made himself captain of one team and
Charles (Bud) Gloo captain of the other. Gloo's boys were
to be known as the Herkimer Businessmen's Nine. Will's
group chose the title YMCA Nine.

All the boys brought baseball uniforms. Baseball long
had been played in Herkimer. Most every lad was equipped
with the accessories for the sport. Someone brought peach
baskets, and Will used the Y's medicine ball. Everything
considered, the boys looked right smart.

But they ran into difficulties as soon as play began.
There were too many boys after the one ball. Will had to
get another. As soon as this was done, the teams paired off
and each played around a basket at opposite ends of the
room.

They threw the ball around, giving the poor peach baskets an awful going-over. When a ball went into a basket, someone had to stand on a chair and take it out. But they had fun. The idea of "basketball" was catching on. They wanted to know more about the sport.

Back at the store, Lambert Will had said something about receiving a pamphlet from a James Naismith who had invented the game. This was the letter that had produced such a peculiar show at Ausman's. The first thing Will did after receiving the pamphlet was to write Naismith for more instructions.

Aside from a few bare outlines of the game that Will had recited to Peterson and Gray that evening, the boys knew nothing about the sport. The truth was that there were no "rules." Letter after letter was sent to Springfield seeking more information. No reply ever came. So Will proceeded on his own. He would give the game rules so it would be playable. He and the boys decided to keep nine men to a side: three "forwards," three "guards," and three "centers."

The medicine ball weighed two and a half pounds. They rolled it along the floor instead of passing it. Will soon had a better idea.

"Boys, this is child's play. I want to try something else. Let's have one from each team come up here to the middle of the floor. I'll throw the ball up and the man that gets the ball plays it from there."

To make it "official," the teams drafted Judge Tom Murray, who happened to be in the hall, to toss up the ball. "Now we have an umpire—just like in baseball," Will said.

The judge took the ball and gingerly tossed it up between the two center rivals. The boys made a grab for the ball and His Honor scooted away. The players began passing the ball around. No one threw it into a peach basket. It became something like "Pass the beanbag." Only rougher. Finally it grew into something akin to rugby. This would never do. Will stopped the game.

"We'll have to work out something better than this," he said. The players picked themselves up from the floor and crowded around their director-coach.

"There isn't any sense to the game as it is now," he said. "We've got to work out some more rules before we play any more." They all agreed. Some rubbed their bruises on shins and elbows. Football was good only on a field, not on a hardwood floor.

"One thing I know right now," said Will. "As long as we're grown-up men, this medicine ball will be thrown around, not rolled."

That was the end of the first practice. Not much accomplished. But it was a start. The "basketball bug" had bitten the players. They were eager to develop the new game. So was Will.

The day after that the boys practiced throwing the ball. They soon found that playing indoors in woolen baseball suits wasn't comfortable. They decided to try bathing suits.

Play commenced. It was almost as rough as it had been the day before and falls, trips, and shoves were frequent. Soon not a man on either side was without floor burns. They were playing on hard maple. So they junked the idea of playing in bathing suits. Instead, they reached a compromise in costume—half and half. The top was bathing suit. The bottom was baseball pants.

But Lambert Will wasn't so much interested in the appearance of his team as in the type of game it played. While the boys experimented with their costumes, he stressed that rules and regulations were necessary. Still no word from Naismith in Springfield. Will would have to continue on his own.

By January 27, 1891, the boys had worked themselves

into enough of a team to want to play a real game. So Tom Murray, the "first" referee, lined up the Businessmen's Nine. They were to play the YMCA Nine.

"Now, how long do you boys want to play?" he asked.

"Until we get tired," was the unanimous answer.

Lambert Will didn't have a better answer. Neither did the judge. So play was begun. The judge tossed up the ball. The boys went at it with a will. The game became very rough. Not only did the players rough each other, but the peach baskets soon were nearly torn from the wall. The game was called until they could be repaired.

Tom Murray pulled out his gold watch. "You've been playing about twenty minutes," he announced.

Everybody rested while the peach baskets were being fixed. Suddenly Will had another idea. Why not remove the bottoms of the baskets so the ball could slide through? That would save a lot of fuss and bother removing the ball each time someone made a basket. Everyone agreed it was a clever idea.

They were ready to resume play. The minutes had passed. Will thought they might as well use twenty minutes as the length of the next period. So they played on. At the end of the second twenty minutes, most of the boys were pretty well done in. Will suggested that they end the game. Everyone agreed. So halves were born because a peach basket only lasted twenty minutes under the pounding of a medicine ball. And the open basket was born because it was too much trouble to stand on a chair and empty the peach basket after each goal.

The second "game" was played the next week, on February 2, 1891. Now that the boys had decided on a definite time period, they were faced with two other problems: how to score each goal and how to penalize unnecessary roughness.

Will decided that a basket thrown from the floor should count three points and that a needless kick, shove, or trip should be called a "personal foul," just as it was in football. When such a foul occurred, the best man on the opposite team should have a free throw at his basket. If he made the throw, it was to count two points.

All right, they agreed, but how far back does one have to stand to make a free throw fair?

It was just a matter of deciding on a fair distance. Will thought six feet was sufficient. The boys thought differently. That would be too easy, they said. And so the distance was lengthened to ten feet. So foul shots and scoring were born.

All these rules came as the need arose. Play had not yet begun. How could it begin until a definite court had been ruled off? Heretofore they had used the confines of the room as boundaries. But there had to be an out-of-bounds somewhere. So they drew a line all around the sides of the YMCA hall six feet out from the wall. If the ball went over this line, it was judged out-of-bounds. If the Y team knocked it out, the Businessmen would resume play with it. This ruling appealed to the players immediately. Will jotted down all the rules that had been decided. Thus was born the basketball court.

So with a combination of football, baseball—and Yankee ingenuity—the game of basketball began to take shape on the floor of the little YMCA. It was a game of expediency first, with each rule made to fit the play as a need became apparent.

But most important, it was a game to occupy the boys during the long, hard, and cold winter evenings. Nothing like it had ever been known. Pitch playing in Em Ausman's General Store couldn't compare to basketball at the Y.

New peach baskets were brought in. Their bottoms were removed. Strong wire was wound around the outsides to keep them from breaking. Because of the low ceilings in the Y, the baskets couldn't be placed any higher than eight feet. It didn't meet with everyone's approval. But it didn't matter. The boys weren't as tall in those days. (The bean pole in basketball is a fairly recent phenomenon.)

In the middle of their new court, they drew a small circle at the suggestion of Tom Murray who wanted to know exactly where he was to begin each game.

The boys agreed that they could take no more than three steps before bouncing or "dribbling" the ball.

The players were assigned definite positions. One center should stand in front, another behind him. The three guards should stand on each side, directly opposite the centers. The forwards were placed down the court in an "offensive" position. Then they were ready to go.

Surveying the anxious youths on the floor, Captain Will was too kind-hearted to offer another obvious suggestion: eighteen players were too many for such a small court. So they played that night with the full squads. It was practice in earnest with rules.

They decided to have a real game next. The date was set for February 7. New, reinforced peach baskets were installed, probably donated by Em Ausman. Judge Murray said he would serve as referee. He had his own whistle.

Lambert Will's mother celebrated her birthday by attending the game. Twenty-five other people, most of them relatives of the players, watched. It was the first actual basketball game ever played in the United States.

The Y team scored a 9 to 3 victory. Judge Murray probably didn't realize it, but he too made history by inaugurating the referee's whistle.

That was the beginning of basketball. Lambert Will

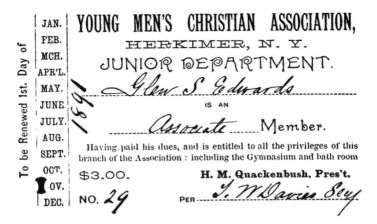

This is a copy of the original 1891 membership card of Glen Edwards of Minoa, N.Y. On Feb. 7, 1891, he witnessed at the Herkimer YMCA the first basketball game ever played.

wrote down all the rules that he and the boys had developed and sent them to James Naismith at Springfield. But as before, no acknowledgment came that they had been received or appreciated. Herkimer went ahead on its own to develop a sport from an idea.

CHAPTER THREE

MR. WILL'S GAME

IT WASN'T LONG before other towns in the Valley heard about the new game that Lambert Will had perfected. They, too, wanted to know how to play basketball. At this first historic game on February 7, 1891, Willard Levee of Little Falls was present. He became so enthusiastic over the new sport that he went back home and organized a team.

Utica, Albany, Syracuse, Troy, and Amsterdam sent representatives to Herkimer to learn all there was to know about "Mr. Will's game." They knew that to have such a thing to offer boys during the long winter would give added interest to YMCA activities.

Will decided Herkimer should have only one nine-man team, now that opposition was growing in other towns. He picked the nine best players from the Y and Businessmen teams, and on the twenty-first they played Mr. Levee's Little Falls team and won by 18–7. It's what you would expect from the original basketball team, isn't it?

Will was the hero of all Herkimer young folk. Especially since he was doing all this without pay. You'll remember that the Y was in financial difficulties after having engaged the services of the physical director.

Will shrewdly realized that the game would lose interest if he confined it to Herkimer. It needed competition from other towns to give a keen sense of rivalry to the sport, to keep it alive and growing.

By now, both Utica and Ilion had teams. Soon Albany sent for the rules. A group of Albany YMCA boys came to see Will. By the end of 1891 Albany had organized a team at their YMCA.

The idea seemed to catch the fancy of Albany newspapers. At least they compared it favorably with football! Here's what one Albany journalist had to say after watching the first Albany team play:

A new game was introduced at the YMCA last evening called "Basketball!" After the floor of the gymnasium was cleared of apparatus, a large bushel basket was hung up on each side of the running track. S. H. Hendricks and E. L. Miller acted as captains and chose sides after ten minutes of lively contesting. Miller's side scored a goal about eight minutes afterwards. Hendrick's boys scored a goal and in about ten minutes the game was decided by a well-aimed throw by one of Miller's men. The game lasted about half an hour, and was voted a decided success and will be tried again Saturday evening. The game has the advantage over football in that it is not as rough, no rushing or tackling being allowed, and the ball is kept in motion by the throwing.

In early February, 1892, the Albany boys became cocky. They issued a challenge to the Herkimer squad. It was to be for the "Basketball Championship of New York State." It was a mythical title then, but both the Albany and the Herkimer boys took the challenge seriously. The Herkimer YMCA Board of Directors accepted the challenge and the game was arranged for February 21.

Will selected his squad with care. There was Simp Peterson (the star), Harry Stanchel, Paul Quackenbush, John Collis, Gorman Harter, and William Wright. Fritz Gray was player-manager. Will was instructor-player and captain.

In the early afternoon of February 21, these nine town heroes made their appearance at the New York Central Station in Herkimer. They were determined to bring home from Albany the "Championship of New York State." They were all togged out in their Sunday best and the whole village bade them farewell. The people were proud to think that these boys had been invited to come to the capital to show their ability.

Yes, sir, they exclaimed, if the town team should return victorious, they would be met by the Herkimer brass band and the hook and ladder company. There would be a great home-coming reception, a torch parade.

The town superintendent of highways and streets promised to remove the snow from Main Street for the parade and the large crowd that was expected. The whole town was excited. And so were the nine men who stood on the platform waiting for the train that would carry them to glory.

At 5:30 that afternoon the Central pulled them into the capital. They were met at the station by members of the Albany team. Greetings were exchanged. Everyone was in a holiday mood. To the small-town boys, Albany was a big city. This was a big occasion.

The Albany team didn't let them forget it. They must go to the Ten Eyck Hotel for dinner, the host team insisted. They had made all the arrangements for a big meal. All expenses would be borne by the locals.

So the Herkimer boys sat down to a sumptuous repast. They acted as though they hadn't eaten in a month. Most of them had never before eaten in a hotel. The Albany boys stood around and seemed to enjoy *just watching* the small-towners eat and eat and eat.

No sooner had the last fork been laid to rest than the big city boys insisted that the Herkimer boys all go for a swim in their new YMCA pool. Flattered to beat the band, the small-towners trooped over to the pool. This was a real treat. They had nothing like this back in Herkimer.

On arriving at the pool, they were so overstuffed with good, rich Ten Eyck food that only one had the ambition to take a swim. He was John Collis, one of Herkimer's best throwers.

The water was very warm. The Albany boys had seen to that. Poor unsuspecting John Collis received a sweat bath. When he dragged himself out of the pool, most grateful to the Albany boys who had allowed him to use their pool, he was so weak he could hardly stand.

But before the small-towners could reflect too much on this state of affairs, they were dragged off to the Y's reception hall. The Herkimer boys could rest here while preparations were being made for the game, said the Albany players.

Oh, by the way, they said, there wasn't any fire in the fireplace. Would some of the Herkimer boys like to split some wood? The woodbox was full of three-foot logs, too big for the fireplace. The Albany boys had seen to that.

Chopping wood was a job with which the Herkimer boys were familiar. In fact, they felt a little superior to the Albany boys in this department. Sure, they would chop some wood. Simp Peterson, six-foot-three giant, weighing two hundred pounds, took the ax and began.

As he was holding one of the logs, the ax head flew from the handle and made a large gash in his left hand. This eliminated Herkimer's star from the contest. Only seven men were fit to play and they were stuffed. The small-towners were becoming suspicious.

Both teams retired to dress in their uniforms. Albany

was represented by nine men. The lineup, as near as can be determined from old journals, was: John Howard Johnson, real estate broker; Supreme Court Justice Harold Hinman; former Commissioner of Welfare Alvin Quental; Roy Heavnor; Fred Phelps; L. H. Hendricks and E. L. Miller, both bankers; LeRoy Parmalee of Delmar; and C. Harry Allen, captain.

The Albany and Herkimer captains decided that nine men on a team were too many anyway. They decided on seven as a good number. The two extra Albany men could be used as substitutes. Of course, Herkimer had no extra men. She had lost her "substitutes" along the way.

Before play could begin, a referee was needed. After some discussion, it was agreed that a referee be chosen from each team. This left six men to play. (The Herkimer referee will be forever nameless.)

The partisan Albany crowd clamored for action. But Will brought up another point. Since Herkimer had lost her center, Peterson, he didn't want a center tap. Herkimer didn't have another tall man. Gorman Harter of Herkimer suggested that instead of the tap, they should take the ball outside the boundary line. When a basket was made by one team, it must present the ball to its opponent, offering them the opportunity to throw the ball back into play. This rule was adopted for this particular game, but was not used afterwards. (Nowadays it is the standard practice; the center jump after every point has been abolished.)

The Albany YMCA hall floor was studded with posts. All week long the Albany players had been practicing and rehearsing what the Herkimer players called hide-and-seek. The Albany boys intended to hide behind the posts when the Herkimer team had the ball and jump out every time a Herkimer man came past. Little did the small-towners know what was in store for them that night!

The referees were chosen. Rocking chairs were provided for them. There weren't too many rules to enforce.

The hall was jammed with sixty Albany rooters. Peach baskets were placed at each end of the hall, but the bottoms were left in. This was so no one could claim the ball didn't go in for a score. Even the referees could be pretty certain, from their chairs, that a basket was made if they saw a player get up on a chair and lift the ball out.

The game resembled football. The referees rocked while the boys socked. The crowd cheered and jeered. The Albany team jumped out from behind the posts at the Herkimer boys and wholly disconcerted them. With more and better manpower, the Albany team soon ran the small-towners ragged. Simp Peterson and John Collis sat glumly on the sidelines and watched as their mates went down to defeat.

The final score was 9–5. The Herkimer team managed to score one basket, which counted three points, and one foul, which counted two. Albany made one basket and three fouls, giving them a total of nine.

By the time the game was over, the Herkimer team had really begun to "smell a rat." They were very displeased with the whole affair. They knew now that the Albany boys were not so dumb. Sure, the city boys had acted like real sports when they invited the small-towners to the Ten Eyck. And what about that swim that knocked the ambition out of John Collis? And that wood-chopping episode that had eliminated their star center?

Hiding behind the posts didn't impress the country lads as being cricket, either. It was a city innovation. They were not in sympathy with it. But this was not the worst. All the foregoing could have been overlooked but for the blame that soon became attached to the referee. You'll remember that the suspicious Herkimer boys had insisted that a referee be chosen from *each* team. The Albany boys had agreed—too easily, the Herkimer boys now began to suspect.

Now the Herkimers were sorry they had picked one of their own members to act as referee. To their astonishment, they found out that the Herkimer boy's lady friend was an Albany girl and that one of the boys on the Albany team was her brother!

As far as the Herkimer boys were concerned, this put the blame where it belonged, right smack on the traitor in their own ranks. They felt that, had they let the Albany referee run the contest, instead of allowing their own lovesick man, they would have had a fairer deal on the matter of fouls.

But alas! Revelation came too late. The game was over. The lover had been true to his lady. The "Championship of New York State" had been lost to the boys at the state capital. And not lost fairly and squarely, either. Sadly the Herkimer boys packed their uniforms and trooped down to the station for the train to Herkimer.

The news of the defeat preceded the train by telegraph back to town. The sad tidings passed around from the station to the general store to the hook and ladder company and to the assembled groups around town. Herkimer had lost!

The band put away its instruments. The members of the hook and ladder company quit their pitch game and went home. The fire died out in Ausman's store. Only the flickering kerosene lights on the village streets greeted the returning team. It was very sad. The superintendent of highways and streets had cleared Main Street for nothing.

Of course, the Herkimer referee was very unpopular. He was asked to leave the team. But the season was not over. The Herkimer boys proved that they could play real ball under normal conditions. With their best players in the lineup and no hide-and-seek games on the side (and a better selection of referees), they went on to play and win nine contests with the Utica YMCA.

Late in 1892 the YMCA in Syracuse organized a team. In January of 1893 the Herkimer team was invited to Syracuse to play in the Y there. This hall was much bigger than the Herkimer hall. The playing space was 60 feet long and 45 feet wide. Peach baskets were up. Lambert Will asked that the bottoms be removed. The Syracusans agreed. Will found that in Syracuse the instructors had tied wire around the baskets to make them rigid just as he had done in Herkimer.

Because of the large floor, the contest was tiresome for Will's boys. It was exceptionally rough, too. However, Herkimer won handily, 12–4.

After the game, the Herkimer boys were so happy that they decided to celebrate. They went over to the Yates Hotel, ordered a bottle of wine, and made merry before boarding the train. Their activities did not go unnoticed. The director-secretary of the Syracuse Y made it his business to report these doings in a letter to Mr. Davies of the Herkimer Y board. The boys from Herkimer, said the Syracusan, were a lot of loafers instead of gentlemen. Y boys should not drink wine. Syracuse would not extend Herkimer another invitation to play because of their "unruly conduct at the Yates Hotel."

This was the end of the Herkimer Y team. The directors decided to disband it.

Lambert Will was very unhappy about the decision of the board. He called a meeting of the team at his home and expressed the hope that they would continue to play somewhere else than at the Y. The boys were eager to maintain their team. Someone suggested they play in the Fox Opera House.

They soon had an agreement for the use of the hall. They had to pay $10 a night rental, plus the expense of burning the gas lights, plus the job of cleaning the hall after each game. The boys agreed.

This was a big undertaking. At the Y there had been no charges. The country was then in a financial panic following the election of Grover Cleveland as President for a second term. Money was scarce. Yet the only solution was to charge an admission fee. Captain Will was given authority to arrange for the first contest and put the Opera House into condition for the game.

Calling themselves now simply the Herkimer Team, the boys extended to the Utica Y the honor of being their first opponents in the opera house. Apparently not in the least abashed at the idea of playing against the ousted Herkimer Y team, the Uticans eagerly accepted the invitation.

The opera house had a ceiling 18 feet high with a floor 80 feet long and 60 feet wide.

The continuing problem of good baskets still plagued the teams. In the hope of a solution, the Herkimer players called in George (Chunky) Volk, the village blacksmith, to see if he could suggest how to make stronger baskets. Chunky came over to the hall and surveyed the scene. Taking one of the peach baskets down, he carted it off to his shop. There he took some steel rods, made a hoop the size of the basket's top, and called in Will, Gray, and Peterson for their opinion. They all were pleased.

The next problem was to fasten it to the wall. Chunky fixed the hoop to a piece of wood with steel clips and fastened it on the wall of his shop. Volk suggested he make a pair of steel arm braces to hold the hoop rigid.

While the boys stood around the blazing forge, Volk

fashioned the first basketball basket frame. It was as solid when finished as an Erie Canal truss bridge.

But Will still felt something was lacking. He thought the bare, sturdy iron hoop had no appeal. He asked for suggestions on how to dress it up. Many were offered by the three. Will himself came up with the best idea. He thought they should hang a netting of some kind around the hoop to give it the appearance of a peach basket. Will was sure his mother could knit a drape to serve the purpose.

So the boys took the iron hoop down and carried it over to Mrs. Will and explained what they wanted. She agreed to do her best to knit two drapes for the hoops. Her undertaking was a success. She made a fine mesh netting. The bottom closed to allow a ball in the net to be seen. A cord hung from the net to open and close the bottom after a basket was made. This innovation was a masterpiece. The boys were delighted. (Even today baskets have drawstrings.)

The next step was for Will to get something other than a medicine ball. Up to this time the team had always used the ponderous ball that Naismith had suggested in his original pamphlet. But it hadn't proved satisfactory. Will decided on something else. In town lived two brothers, Joe and Mose Schermer, who were star rugby players. They owned a rugby ball. Will asked if he might borrow it. The brothers agreed. Chunky Volk agreed to enlarge his hoops for the new ball. The team used the rugby ball for the rest of the season.

Compared to modern basketballs, this rugby ball was crude. The problem of a good ball was not solved until late in the twenties. Up to then, the balls did not hold their shape long. That's one big reason for low scores in early basketball. You just couldn't dribble and shoot with a lopsided ball.

The new baskets with their knitted drapes were hung in the opera house. They were placed ten feet above the floor this time, because the new hall was so much higher than the old Y court. The players found it was much easier to make baskets in the new hoops than it had been in peach baskets. Higher scores were the result. The game was dressed up compared to the old setup.

Chalk lines indicated the foul shooting position, now placed fifteen feet in front of the basket. The center circle was drawn and a boundary line was marked along the sides of the court, leaving enough space for spectators.

Village folks, forgetting their disappointment over the debacle in Albany, became enthusiastic over the preparations being made at the opera house for the game with Utica. Folding chairs were brought in to accommodate 150.

The Utica team arrived on a cold January day. A few fans came along on the train with them. They were amazed at the size of the opera house court—34 by 50 feet.

Rules for that game called for seven men on a team. Two extra players could be used as subs. The Uticans agreed. One player from each team could act as referee. (The Herkimer boys were very careful in the selection of a referee this time.)

A 20-cent admission fee was charged, yet every one of the 150 folding chairs was occupied at game time. As a result, Will insisted on paying the Uticans' expenses.

Utica wore baseball uniforms. The Herkimer team had on baseball pants, long stockings, sneakers and bathing tops.

The contest was rather rough. But it was nothing to compare to the YMCA games. Herkimer won 16–5. Baskets still counted three, fouls two. The game was of twenty-minute halves with a ten-minute rest. There were timekeepers. (The life of those original peach baskets was to govern a basketball period for many years.)

It was the first professional basketball game in the United States. The Herkimer boys each took home some change after paying their own and Utica's expenses.

In spite of the economic situation, the loss of Y support, and the fact that the players had to make the rules as they went along, basketball became firmly established in Herkimer and the Valley. Ingenuity and a desire to perfect an exciting game conquered all. The fever spread. Before the season of 1893 ended, Herkimer played another game at Syracuse, this time at the Alhambra Hall. This hall had a floor 90 by 40 feet. Ninety feet was a long way between baskets. The exhausting game ended in a 6–6 tie. Before the final whistle, it had almost become a question of which boys could stand the relay running on such a long floor.

Charles McCormick, Syracuse captain, and Warren Rullison, Herkimer captain, did not know what to do. This situation had never occurred before. Rullison made a suggestion. He offered to wrestle McCormick, no holds barred, to decide the winner of the game. The first man thrown on his back with his shoulders to the floor would lose.

Both removed their uniform tops. McCormick saw the mighty muscles on Rullison. He decided there must be a better way to finish the game. After all, it would look rather foolish for a man from a big city like Syracuse to be beaten by a man from a little town like Herkimer. McCormick suggested they ought to call the game a tie and let it go. Rullison finally was persuaded to put on his shirt again. It was understood they would play the game over again sometime.

But the ever-resourceful Lambert Will stepped up with a suggestion. Ties were likely to occur again and again. It would be better if they decided then and there what to do.

He suggested playing overtime five minutes. The team that was ahead then would win. The players agreed. Herkimer scored a basket and won 9–6.

By 1894 Ilion had a team. In New York City the 23rd Street Y formed one. In 1895 Troy and the 44th Separate Company of Schenectady had squads, along with the Binghamton Y, the 7th Separate Company of Cohoes, the Central Y of Philadelphia, and Camden, N. J.

In and around Philadelphia there were a hundred teams by 1901 when William J. Scheffer organized the first Philadelphia basketball league. All the players were paid a salary. The A.A.U. at the time wanted to tax each player 25¢ apiece for membership and $1.50 for the team. But Scheffer won out in the battle to keep the teams professional. In 1909 this league became the Eastern League with Trenton, Camden, Reading, Jasper, Greystoke, and DeNeri. Scheffer was president from 1901 to 1930.

In 1894 the New York State Armory was completed at Mohawk across the river from Herkimer. Lambert Will decided to move the team to this larger arena. Arrangements were made with Captain Whiterstein. The Armory would receive 50 per cent of net receipts, the team 50 per cent.

As more and more teams organized throughout the Valley, they were invited to play the famous Herkimer team in the new Mohawk Armory. With its removal to the Armory, the team changed its name to the 31st Separate Company. Their first game under this name was at Little Falls in November, 1894, in the old Arcadia Rifle Corps Hall. Seven hundred jammed the house. Herkimer won 28–8.

The next week, on Thanksgiving night, the same Little Falls team, known as the Athletics, was invited to play in the Armory. The Herkimer team set about getting ready for the big game. A new rugby ball was secured. But when the boys began to practice with the new ball, they found something wrong. They had placed their iron baskets directly against the brick walls of the Armory. Every time a shot at the basket missed, the more lively new ball would bound off the brick wall with a great deal of speed. Lambert Will suggested that the boys build a wooden platform behind the basket to deaden the shots.

Some of the boys liked the idea of making shots "clean," but the rest decided, in the interest of higher scores, that a "backboard" would be a good idea. The iron baskets were removed and brought down to Diemel and Snell's lumber yard. Since it was Thanksgiving Day and they did not have to work, the entire team went along. The mill operator, Peter Heinzelman, who did have to work, agreed to build a backboard for the team. When it was completed, the boys placed studs behind it to bring it away from the wall. Then they carried it over to Mohawk in Frank Munson's two-seated cutter.

The boys found that the addition of backboards made shooting much easier. They practiced most of the afternoon on the re-bound shot.

The game with Little Falls would inaugurate basketball in the Armory. There were seats for 1800 and another 200 could stand. The floor was 80 by 60 feet. There were two balconies, and there were both bleachers and stationary seats. The American flag was draped inside and there was a large glass case displaying Remington rifles. Admission was 35 cents.

Three hundred Little Falls fans came on special West Shore coaches to see the game. Others came by sleigh.

Before the game, the teams agreed to use the center jump, abolishing the rule made at Albany in 1892 that the team scored on should take the ball out of bounds. This game was the first in which there were five men on a side.

The two extra guards were used as substitutes. The smallest man on each team jumped center. This was to avoid unfair advantage if one team had a giant and the other team didn't. Tink Metzger of Herkimer stood 5 feet, 5 inches. Frank Ottman of Little Falls stood 5 feet, 6. These two were considered the fastest players in the valley.

In those days, only the most violent body contact was penalized—quite unlike the game today when the slightest unintentional brush can be (and usually is) called a foul. There were two referees, one from each team. The game was rough, but the referees didn't have much to do. It was more like hockey than what we know as basketball now. Herkimer won 22–6. Little Falls did not score a point in the second half. This was also the first game in which a field goal counted two points and a free-throw, one.

In 1895 the basketball rules committee was organized with Sandy Shields of New York as chairman. Rules worked out by this group were exactly the same as those developed by the Herkimer boys in 1891.

On April 2, 1896, Herkimer and Cohoes played a famous game in the Armory. Herkimer lost the game, 10–8, but there was some argument over the affair. This is how a newspaper described it:

SEVENTH AND THIRTY-FIRST COMPANIES' BASKETBALL GAME UNSATISFACTORY

Herkimer, April 2—There never has been as rough or unfair a game of basketball played at the Armory as that put up by the Seventh Company team of Cohoes in the game with the Thirty-First Separate Company team last night. From the start the Cohoes referee seemed determined to give the visitors the best of it. Whenever the Thirty-First team got the ball anywhere near their goal, a foul was almost sure to be called, and to cap the climax, there seems to be no doubt in the world but that the Cohoes timekeeper set his watch three minutes ahead. When the game started the watches of both timekeepers were alike and when time was called in the last half they were three minutes apart, the Cohoes timekeeper's watch being three minutes ahead. All through the last half the Cohoes referee played for time holding the ball just as long as possible whenever he got it in his hands.

In the first half the visiting team got a lead of five, the score standing 8 to 3 in their favor. In the last half the home team scored 5 to the visitors' 2, making the final score 10 to 8 in favor of the Cohoes team. The local team outplayed the visitors all through the last half, and if fair ball had been played, or even if the home team had played the kind of ball played by the visitors, the outcome would have been decidedly different.

When it became known that the timekeepers' watches varied three minutes, it was all the cool heads could do to avert the warmest kind of a row. . . .

In 1895 Herkimer produced the first high school team. Edwin J. Beckingham was manager. The boys called themselves the "Juniors" or the "High School Five." They played in the Fox Opera House now that the older men were using the new Armory. The Juniors followed the same rules used by the former Y team.

Other high schools also formed teams. Soon there was much scholastic competition in the Valley. In those days schools didn't have expensive gymnasiums as they do today. The kids used anything from church halls to town halls in which to play their games.

The game soon went higher scholastically. Hamilton College at Clinton was probably the first college to organize a team. It lost its first game to Herkimer 42–8.

The nation's top team in 1897 was the 23rd Street Y of New York. It continued to be one of the best until 1902. Sandy Shields, their captain, became to basketball then what Babe Ruth later became to baseball. The team played practically all its games on the road and had no equal at the box-office.

Besides Shields (who held the world's foul shooting rec-

ord of thirty-three consecutive shots), there were Kid
Eberlien, Bobby Grief, Eddie Wendelkein, Bill Reid, Bob
and Turk Abadie, and Dutch Detrich.

Other well-known teams of the '90s were the East Liver-
pool, Ohio, Five, the 15th Separate Company of Pough-
keepsie, the 4th Separate Company of Yonkers, the Washington Heights team, the Silent Five (deaf mutes) of New
York, and the Castleton Five of West Brighton, N. Y.

But Herkimer's own 31st Separate Company was the
champion of them all. In 1900 they won the New York
State Championship after defeating the 23rd Street Y, the
Silent Five, and teams throughout the Mohawk Valley.

In that year George Sluyter was manager, Lambert Will
was captain. Others were Harry Stanchel, George Swart-
out, Tink Metzger, Fred Gray, and Toby Smith.

The great Toby Smith was working for his father on
the family homestead. Like all farmers, Toby had to do
his share of the chores before he could play basketball.
Toby lived on "Hungry Hill," two miles from Herkimer.
He told Lambert Will how one night he was almost late
because one of the cows had udder trouble. After doctor-
ing her, Toby had to chop a shed full of kindling wood before he was allowed to take the horse and cutter to the
Armory for the game that night. He chopped enough
wood that Saturday to keep the fires going under every
bathtub in Herkimer. Toby got to the game on time,
played his usual great style, danced until midnight with
his best girl, and got back to Hungry Hill at 2. He was up
the next morning at 4:30 for chores. This was not an unusual performance for Toby. Herkimer played a couple
of games each week.

Lambert Will had played with the Rifle Corps team at
Little Falls and had traveled with the Silent Five of New
York as a lip reader. For two summers he had traveled as

a rube acrobat, once with the Breezy Times and another with the Sig Sautelle Circus.

A few years later Lambert was offered a chance to play with the 23rd Street team in New York, but he decided he didn't want to play on the road anymore. He became a cartoonist for Tommy Gaffney's labor paper in Syracuse, and later, in 1910, opened a print shop in Little Falls. He retired from this business in 1948 and went to live with his son on a small farm in Nelson, N. Y. Will is the oldest professional basketball player in the country.

In 1898 the team lost Lambert Will when he enlisted for service in the Spanish-American War. Two years later George Sluyter resigned as manager and Bill Hartigan took over. The new team consisted of Toby Smith, Tink Metzger, and Simp Peterson from the 1900 team. New players were Strings Caswell, Turk Daly, and George Shoemaker. This team disbanded in 1903, but several of its players joined Simp Peterson, the greatest center in the game from 1891 to 1902, to form a new club that established a record of 64 won and 7 lost in three years. This new team had on it two sets of brothers, Simp Peterson and Babe Peterson, and the Murname twins, Ed and Jim. Jim later traveled with the Globe Trotters throughout the West and became an all-time great basketball star.

So basketball got its start. It was a lusty, strapping youngster by 1903. It had advanced a long way from that Christmas in 1890 when Lambert Will hustled into Em Ausman's General Store with a pamphlet in his pocket, an idea in his head, and a determination to make something work.

Basketball became a kind of social hot-stove league in the valley. Dancing would always follow games, which were usually over by 10 o'clock. Boys and girls made their own fun at these after-game affairs. The married population of Herkimer rose steadily with the rise of basketball.

EXPERTS AT BASKETBALL.

Herkimer Crack Players Have Lost But Two of Thirty-five Games.

Herkimer, Feb. 19.—The Thirty-first Separate company basket ball team, of the reorganized Herkimer Y. M. C. A. team, the change being made about a year ago. It is doubtful if there is another team in the State that can have as large a percentage of games won.

For seven years the team has met all comers. Besides winning fresh laurels in every field the team has been very successful in financial matters. It has been self-supporting and has aided a number of teams playing under the name of Herkimer Juniors.

In the fall of 1891 the Herkimer Y. M. C. A. organized a basket ball team, which was believed would do credit to the association, and it was not long before they were the undisputed champions of Central New York. The players in 1891 were: Will, captain; Collis, Peterson, Stansel, Gray, Steel and Schmidt. The first four named play with the team to-day and have played in every game since the team was organized. Although they played a very clever game it was not possible to win at all times, and in 1892 they lost the banner, being defeated by the Albany Y. M. C. A. team. In 1893, under the captaincy of Frank Peterson, the Herkimer boys again won the championship.

In 1894 "Link" Metzger was taken onto the team, first as a substitute and then as a regular player. His position is center, and it would be hard to find his equal as a good thrower. Collis and Will, the forwards of the team, are very active, their passing, combined with Metzger's long throws, is a feature of every game. Frank Peterson and Harry Stansel, who is captain of the team, can always be relied upon in their position as guards, never having had more than 14 points thrown over them, and that number only once. They can almost be called the main stay of the team. Smith, the first substitute, has proven himself a first-class player. Warren Rulison, manager of the team, has held that position since 1896, and has shown great ability for the place.

This is the team's first year with five men, they always having played with seven heretofore. Since the team was organized in 1891, they have played thirty-five games, of which they have only lost two. Once to the Albany Y. M. C. A. and once to the Thirty-seventh Separate company of Schenectady. Some of the teams they have won from are: The Forty-fourth Separate company of Utica, one game; the Forty-sixth Separate company of Amsterdam, one game; the Syracuse Y. M. C. A., two games and one tie; the Utica Y. M. C. A., eight games and one tie; the West Troy Y. M. C. A., one game; the Ilion Y. M. C. A., four games; the Ilion Athletics, two games; the Little Falls Athletics, four games; the Herkimer Kappa Gamma Chi, one game, and the Herkimer Business Men, one game.

The team has only had two managers, Gray, from 1891 until 1896, and Rulison, from 1896 up to date. The team has had three captains: Lambert Will, 1891; Frank Peterson, from 1892 until 1897, and Harry Stansel, the present captain. The team is noted as always playing a fair and gentlemanly game.

Copy of a news article which appeared in the Utica Daily Press, Utica, N.Y., Feb. 19, 1898, containing evidence that basketball was played in Herkimer, N.Y., in 1891.

Winter came early in those days. By the middle of October the hills were white. The season opened about November 15. By then it was nothing to have four feet of snow. Fans came to the games on cutters, bobs, and wagons. Most of them tied up at the "Montana House" across the way from the Mohawk Armory. With a half-pint in their pockets, they stayed warm. The cold seldom kept attendance down. The horse cars crossing the river from Herkimer were always loaded with happy citizens. At times the Armory was so jammed that daring spectators climbed out onto the rafters to see. There were no taxes on games then. Players and managers divided the profits equally. Life then was plainer, simpler—and a little bit more honest. The people were as young in heart as basketball was young in years.

CHAPTER FOUR

...INTO HIGH-TONED
AMERICANS

IT WAS very hot in the summer of 1891 when the ship carrying my mother, my sister Fannie, and myself steamed into New York Harbor. Old Lady Liberty never held her lamp higher than that day I first saw her against the skyline.

It was the same year the first basketball game had been played in Herkimer. But I, Frank Basloe, knew nothing of basketball nor of Herkimer. I was only four and deathly sick from eating too many American doughnuts. The rolling of the ship plus the heavy food almost ended my career before I landed.

We stood together looking out over the misty harbor at the tall buildings of New York. Somewhere deep in the heart of this new land was the village of Herkimer. In this new village my father, Josef Breslau (as we were known then), had found work, had a home for us, had established himself like so many immigrants before him. Now he had sent for his family in Vienna.

It had been a hard trip. Leaving the banks of the Danube in the burning heat of summer, the three of us had begun the 3000-mile trip West. Just a year earlier Papa had taken the same trip. He had heard of the new land, the opportunities, the freedom that were to be had in America. He had left his pregnant wife and little son behind and set out to make his fortune.

At Ellis Island he had been told there was work in the mines at Scranton. My father's military training in Europe had made a good marcher out of him. So he set out on foot. He reached Scranton four days later. But there was no work. It had been a false report. He couldn't speak, read, or write English. But he was not alone. Other immigrants were there faced with the same grim future—work or starve. They had heard of a railroad being built somewhere north of Scranton. The town's name was Herkimer.

Once again my father set out on foot. He reached Herkimer in a week. For the first time since landing, he found work. The Mohawk and Malone Railroad was being built; there was a job at $6 a week.

Herkimer had other immigrants. Papa found friends, Italians by the name of Lorraine. They offered him room and board. From then on, my father worked steadily and hard toward the day that he could send for his family back in Austria. Steamship tickets were expensive. His small salary didn't go far. But he kept saving.

Finally in June, 1891, with the help of the Jewish Aid Society, Mother got the tickets and the money with which to make the journey to join her husband. Fannie and I were tagged like cattle at a fair. First stop was Paris. Here near disaster came upon us. Mother lost the passports. We were detained at the House of Rothschild offices until the matter was straightened out. Once again tagged, we left for the coast and soon were on board ship for America.

One doesn't remember too much from the age of four. All that I knew was that I was on a long and tiring journey. I remember getting sick in New York Harbor. I vaguely remember the Statue of Liberty there to greet the boat. I remember the tall buildings in the distance, the hustle of Ellis Island. And I remember the terrible time we had because my mother's cousin who owned a New York department store wasn't at the Island to meet us.

Three homeless immigrants were stranded in the new land. With the help of sympathetic immigration officials, we got to the mainland. The Jewish Aid Society again stepped in. We were given tickets to Herkimer on the New York Central.

There, I remember, a nice man met us at the station. He kissed my mother. It was Papa. He could hardly believe the little boy in the Austrian velvet suit and cap was his son. He had never seen Fannie.

Together again and very happy, the four of us went off to our new home on Stimson Street which Papa had rented for $4 a month. Papa told Mama how he had been living with the Lorraines on Dewey Avenue. She was very disturbed to think he had almost forgotten the good food she used to prepare for him. Papa assured her that he had not lost his taste for her cooking.

We were something of a curiosity to the people of Herkimer as we marched down the streets that day with our foreign clothes and luggage. But Papa had made a good name for himself. They were glad to see the rest of his family.

Before our arrival, Father had done a great deal of shopping. New dishes, silverware, cooking utensils, and food were stacked in the house on Stimson Street. Mama was delighted. The first task she set herself was to prepare a meal such as Papa had not tasted in a year and a half. There was pickled herring, chicken noodle soup with lots of noodles, matzo balls, boiled chicken cooked in vegetables, and for dessert some real apple strudel. Along with this we had real tea with lemon and some of Mrs. Louis Schermer's home-made bread. Now Mama knew America was a good land.

In a year I was going to school. We had settled down to life in America. The boy next door, Adam Allen, became my chum. He took me that first day to meet Miss Margaret Tuger, the teacher. Everyone was very nice to me. After classes, I met Paul Greiner and Clinton Griffin. These three new playmates set about making an American of me. It didn't take long, either.

In two years we moved to an old house on the corner of South Washington and East Smith Street. There was a small barn in the back. I was to play my first basketball in this barn. Out back were a few apple trees. All this rented for $6 a month.

Papa worked now in Diemel and Snell's Lumber Yard for $8 a week. The salary wasn't enough to pay for a new roof on our house. When it rained, the water came into our bedrooms upstairs. At night we would have to move to drier quarters below. For a kitchen floor we had wide rough-hewn planks with cracks in between. These cracks were wide enough to let rats through. What my father called his favorite indoor sport was killing these intruders with a homemade slap-stick. So our life went.

Our kind friend Louis Schermer gave us a Jersey cow, and another neighbor, Will Schrader, gave Papa twenty chickens. We raised most of our vegetables, having to buy only sugar, salt, flour, coffee, and the few other things we couldn't raise ourselves. In the fall we harvested cabbages, potatoes, carrots, beans, squash, corn, and tomatoes. Mama would begin canning, a favorite chore with her. Papa's job was to make the sauerkraut, shredding the heads in a big vinegar barrel, salting them, and then stamping them. We used to put about four dozen apples on top of the shredded cabbage when it had begun to ferment. We ate well in the new land.

Early one spring a few years later, Mother took Papa's lunch to him at the lumber yard. She had a new baby then, little Sarah, who rode in the carriage with Fannie. I tagged along behind. At the yard, we saw Papa rolling the big logs around by hand. It was very hard work. He was sweating in the spring sunshine that day. Mama made up her mind that this heavy labor would not continue.

That night when Papa came home from work with his cap on and his blotched coat under his arm, Mama announced that he was not to work in the lumber yard any more. It was too hard work.

"You have worked hard enough Yusel," she said. "Back in the old country you hired out to fight for a rich man's son in the Turk war, but in America you should not have to live so hard. You should be able to work less. There is much opportunity in America. You will not work so hard."

Soon Father was convinced that Mama was right. Mama and Papa had $400. First, they bought the house we lived in on South Washington Street for $1400 with $200 down and the balance at $8 a month with 6 per cent interest. Next, Papa built himself a small building on Washington Street and opened up a store. He planned to sell candy, school supplies, and some groceries. There were no other stores nearby. The South Side School was directly across the street. There were kids enough to buy his goods. But the new store cost him $200, the remainder of his savings. His problem was how to buy the supplies needed to stock the store.

Papa went off to see Frank Sphon, a successful grocer in Herkimer where he had been trading. Papa outlined his problem. Frank agreed to help. Although it meant setting up a small competitor, the kindly grocer agreed to stock the little store from his own shelves.

There was still a great deal of room for more stock. Papa went to his other good friend John McKennan, manager of the Grange Exchange, the largest store of its kind in Herkimer County. Without hesitation Mr. McKennan agreed to help stock the new store. The bill? Oh, that could be paid when the stock was sold. So Father got his start with $400 and two generous good neighbors.

In a month Papa quit his job at the lumber yard. Mama had run the store in the meanwhile. Business was good. It wasn't long before the two debts were paid off. My father, Frank Sphon, and John McKennan became fast friends. One time when Mr. McKennan was sick in the hospital, my father closed his store to go and see him. That was a memorable occasion, because Papa never left the store unless it was to go to the bank or for a beer at Bartley Manion's place.

In 1897 I was ten. I found that of all our sports—skating, baseball, football, and basketball—I liked basketball best. It was *the* sport in Herkimer. The famous 31st Separate Company team was beating all opponents down at the new Mohawk Armory. The players became my heroes.

In the barn out back of our house we kids put up a wooden hoop from a flour barrel. Mother made us a basketball out of rags left over after she had made a crazy quilt. We had great fun that winter throwing our "ball" through the hoop.

One day the kids asked me to go with them to see a real basketball game at the Armory. I asked Mama. She agreed. We kids had no money to pay the admission fee. We intended to sneak in. Off we went along the Mohawk River to the Armory. There we walked around to the side of the building and squeezed in through one of the basement windows. We landed on the coal pile inside. By the time we got up to the playing floor, all smudged with coal dust, the game was half over.

The Armory was jammed. The 31st was playing Little Falls. It was thrilling to see them pass the beautiful leather rugby ball back and forth with such ease and precision. Someday I hoped I too would own a leather rugby ball. The game ended with our heroes the victors.

We continued to play in the barn with renewed interest. I met other boys who liked basketball. Our little barn on Washington Street was too small to hold the crowds. We switched playing floors to the Hall barn on Eastern Avenue. Each boy got his mother to make him a rag ball like mine.

Sometimes we would play in empty box cars on the sidings in the Herkimer yards. One day while we were doing this, the car in which we were playing was picked up by an engine and started on a journey to Malone. Just for the heck of it, we went along for the ride as far as Remsen. Then we hitched a ride back on another train. In those days trains went slow enough so that you could hop them. Of course, if you missed your hold and fell, you would get a face full of cinders.

Soon I had learned the names of all the 31st's players: Simp Peterson, Tob Smith, Tink Metzger, Lambert Will, Fritz Gray, and George Sluyter, the manager. We kids organized teams of our own. The North Siders against the South Siders. Outside of the 31st team, we played the best basketball in Herkimer. On our team were the Murnane twins, Jim and Ed, future stars.

Papa's business was flourishing. I got a little extra candy if Papa wasn't looking; so I was popular with the boys.

I still dreamed of owning a leather basketball of my own. I got a job selling *Utica Saturday Globe* newspapers in town about the time I was fourteen. The paper offered a prize for the most papers sold that year. There were a pair of boots, a football, a pair of ice skates and—a real, leather basketball made by Spalding, just like the one the 31st Separate Company used.

I boosted the circulation of the *Saturday Globe* quite a lot that year. I won first prize. The leather basketball became mine. I worked so hard and so long hawking newspapers, though, that my school work suffered. I failed my examinations. My teacher told Papa. But he wasn't concerned. He was busy setting up a junk yard, and Mama was busy taking in pack peddlers as boarders. The feel of my own money in my pocket was too much. I couldn't see going to school when I could make money selling papers. Although I remained in school, I did not advance any further than the sixth grade.

I remember one day I was sitting in class in the school building which was directly across the street from Papa's store. My teacher called me over to the window facing the store.

"Frank, has your father sold out?" she asked.

"Not that I know of," I replied.

"But look at that new sign on his store. It says 'Joe Basloe'."

"Well, I can't help it," I said. "My father owned the store when I left this morning."

After school I went over to the store to find out.

"Did you sell the store, Papa?"

"I should say not," he said.

"But look at the sign out front."

We both stepped outside and looked. "That isn't the way to spell our name," I said. "That says Joe Basloe."

Josef Breslau, who could neither read nor write, looked

at the sign and said: "That's my name, all right. Who knows better than me?"

So overnight my father became Joe Basloe. The same thing happened to many of the people who immigrated to the new land.

Although most of the boys in our gang had to sneak into the Armory through the coal bin to see the 31st play, there were some lucky ones who didn't. Kids like the Murnane twins, Babe Peterson, Charles Greiner, Crump Clark, and Bummy Bowers were the big team's favorites. They were allowed to carry the hero's bags into the game, thus getting in free. They were the envy of all of us other kids.

In 1900 the 31st had changed and George Sluyter was replaced by Bill Hartigan as manager. Fritz Gray also resigned. The team took on String Caswell of Ilion and Turk Daly of Mohawk. The boys who carried the players' bags were allowed to play a preliminary game before the main event. This released six positions for new bag carriers. I was one of the lucky ones. Lambert Will, my favorite player, let me carry his bag onto the floor. That was a big moment in my little life.

Soon I, too, was practicing on the Armory floor. I brought my new leather basketball and some of the kids who had played in our barn.

Later when Lambert Will signed to play with the Silent Five of New York, I got to carry Turk Daly's bag. Soon people started to come early to see the kids' teams in action. You might say this was the first time we played before a real audience.

So in nine years the Basloes had made progress. Father's store was doing very well. He became a frequent depositor at the bank. His progress was a matter of pride for the whole family. I remember one story told about him. Father Halpin of St. Francis de Sales Church had offered my father a job as janitor of his church when father first came to Herkimer. But because Father couldn't read or write, he didn't get the job. After he became successful in business, he was endorsing his check with an X in the bank one day when Tod McCreery, the treasurer, looked up at him and said, "Joe, it's too bad you can't read and write; just think what you might have been."

Father thought a minute and then said, "Yes, if I could read and write, I would have been the janitor of the Catholic Church."

Our back yard was commencing to show the effects of an expanding junk business. We children didn't like it at all. We felt the junk business was beneath us. The problem cleared itself up one day when a pack of noisy urchins from the North Side came by my father's store yelling at the top of their voices, "Any rags, any bones, any bottles today? Old Joe Basloe is coming this way."

It was but a short time after this that Father sold every bit of junk he had. He also made Mother give up taking in pack peddlers for boarders. We were no longer immigrants; we were now high-toned Americans.

CHAPTER FIVE

I BECOME THE FIRST "GLOBE TROTTER" AT SIXTEEN

ONE DAY in February, 1903, I was rummaging around in an old church my father had just bought. He was going to make it over into a two-family house. In the attic I found an old Montreal newspaper. It had stories of basketball games played in the north country. Listed were Ogdensburg, Malone, Lake Placid, Saranac Lake, Tupper Lake, and Fort Covington.

I decided to become a basketball promoter.

I was sixteen years old and in the sixth grade. I trooped over to the local printer in Herkimer and ordered some fancy letterheads which I could pay for with some of the money I'd earned selling papers and Tanglefoot fly paper. They carried the legend: "Herkimer Team—Champions of the Mohawk Valley."

I sent letters to all the northern towns which had teams and asked them for games. It worked. The fancy letterheads impressed the northerners. I had a schedule of six games by the last week in February.

To look like an established business man, I bought myself a $12-suit, a wing collar, a black fore-in-hand necktie, and a 10¢ pearl stick pin. Now that I had a schedule and

46

a wardrobe, I set about looking for the "championship team" that I had advertised.

Even at the age of sixteen, I was well aware that the basketballers in the North Woods would provide rough and tough opposition. That's why I picked Lew Wachter and Jimmy Williamson at $5 each a game. I left the great Ed Wachter home because he came too high at $10 a game.

Lew and Jimmy had played their first games with the Troy, N.Y., YMCA. Later they joined the Columbia A.C. and played in the Western Massachusetts Basketball League. At the time I asked for their services, they were playing for the Co. E team of Schenectady.

I wrote Lew and Jimmy letters outlining my plans for a road trip north and asking them if they would be interested in joining my "champions."

Sure, Lew wrote back. He was a nineteen-year-old wonder on the court. But, he said, I would have to send him an advance of $4 for "expenses." This was in the event that his journey from Troy to Herkimer turned out to be some brand of fool's errand. I remember that at the time I thought it was very queer for him to want his money in advance. But I learned fast. Being a promoter is one of the quickest ways to "get wise" to the world.

Four dollars was a lot of money. What's more, I didn't have it. Lew wouldn't come unless I sent it, and I needed him badly. It was just before Christmas. Everyone in Herkimer was in a holiday frame of mind. "Merry Christmasses" floated out over the valley air with the wood smoke. People were in a generous mood.

I started out to raise four dollars. I crunched through the snow to the door nearest my home and knocked. A man answered. I swept off my cap and wished him a very Merry Christmas and a Happy New Year. The man was so surprised by this cherub-like greeting that he fished down into his jeans and came up with a dime. That left $3.90 to raise.

There were plenty of houses in Herkimer. And plenty of people. The night was cold, the snow was falling, the streets were dimly lit. But I set out determined to increase my endowment. By ten o'clock (when most of the good citizens of Herkimer turned down their lamps, went to bed, and forgot Christmas) I had accumulated $3 in silver. After ten o'clock it wouldn't have been wise to rap on doors. I went home. One dollar more and I was a real promoter.

The next day I decided to help Papa in the store. This was unusual. He was quite surprised. Most of the time I was out playing basketball. Since it was holiday time, Papa felt generous and came across with a pair of racing skates. I sold them for $2. Now my operating capital showed a surplus. Papa didn't know about my northern trip.

I sent Lew Wachter the $4, and he and Jimmy Williamson took the first train for Herkimer. I contacted the Murnane twins, Ed and Jim, in Herkimer, asking them if they too would like to play on a "championship" team. They agreed. So I finally had my team (I was to be fifth man). I used the extra dollar to buy myself a basketball uniform.

Then the day came when I needed five tickets to Ogdensburg, the first town on our schedule. The trip was to last six days and include, besides Ogdensburg, Malone, Tupper Lake, Saranac Lake, Lake Placid, and Fort Covington. I needed money again.

Since I knew my father would never let me go on such a trip, I went to my mother for assistance. I told her I was leaving for a day for the north country and asked her to lend me $10. (Although Papa could talk in seven different languages, when I asked him for money he never could understand me.) But Mother—well, most mothers are alike. I sat down and had a heart-to-heart talk with Mother. She went to the cupboard. But the cupboard was bare. Then she went into a corner, stooped down, and took $10 from the top of her stocking.

I promised to pay it back. After all, I was her only son and going into business. She pressed my suit and put clean underwear in my bundle. I felt as if I were going to cross the ocean again. She also agreed to see Papa and explain my absence. He was given to understand I was going to spend the day and evening in Utica with Solly Goldbas whom my father considered a good boy. You see, Mother didn't know this jaunt north was to take six days. Soon we were chugging along to Ogdensburg.

The Ogdensburg team was made up of tough Irish boys who called themselves the "fighting Irish." (Before we got home, I had about decided that all basketball players in the north country were Irishmen.) Once they gave you a knock, you really felt it. But we gave it right back to them. My team played like champions. And this was the first time that Wachter and Williamson and the Murnane twins had ever seen each other.

We passed the ball around so fast I think that the crowd got dizzy watching it. I played what was called standing back guard. The boys thought that would be the best position for me because of my big flat feet. I looked good in practice and made some shots that never touched the rim of the hoop, but I wasn't really supposed to shoot. Still, I told myself, if I felt like shooting a basket now and then, who could stop me? I was the manager, timekeeper, and coach of the outfit, wasn't I?

We won that first road game 16–10. Our guaranteed purse was $75. Out of this I paid each of the boys his $5 and bought them breakfast the next morning. Did those Irishmen on *my* team know how to eat! They had ham and bacon and eggs. All I had was eggs.

The next night in Saranac, we won 24–13. My team had spirit. The Murnane twins shot so well that they hardly ever touched the rims. Jim was a fighter. Nobody dared start any rough stuff with him. Eddie was a wonderful shot. Jimmy Williamson and Lew Wachter were just as good.

From my position as standing guard, I started all the plays. When the other team had the ball, it was my job to watch the boy who had it. I also watched the finances and the timekeeper.

We played in the Opera House at Saranac Lake. Among the spectators were a group of girls our own age. They were beauties who could have won prizes anywhere as models. We were filled with pity when we learned that they all had "consumption." We met them after the game and had a nice visit—after the doctors had assured us the disease wasn't catching. I remember I wished I was older so I could marry one of the girls and then try to make her happy. They enjoyed the game. They said that with a team such as ours no one could beat us. They were right, too.

Our next stop was Tupper Lake on Monday night. The Frenchmen there were the toughest Canadians anyone ever met. But we were finally victorious by 16–10.

We beat Company K of Malone 20–12 next. Malone was a nice place, but it was awfully cold. The townspeople said the only difference between Alaska and Malone was five thousand miles. We did a great deal of riding in sleighs with lots of belles, but we still needed lots of blankets to keep us warm.

Our schedule took us to Fort Covington next. We beat them 24–20. I don't think there were over ten boys who lived in the town. We had to go in by sleigh. Fort Covington had only about a thousand people. But they had one of the fastest basketball teams in the state.

We played at beautiful Lake Placid the next night. The

man who ran the team was a Mr. Stevens—a big man with a big hotel. He had two sons as big as John L. Sullivan. They both played on the team. But in spite of this and the fact that the hall for the game was very small, we won 18–12. Jim Murnane, our star, said I stood too long in one place. But with the wad that was growing in my red handkerchief, I didn't think I was standing still. I had made almost $300.

After the game, Mr. Stevens insisted on another contest. We were staying at his hotel and he invited us down to the living room for an egg eating contest.

The two teams would be matched to see which could eat the most eggs. Well, I had signed my team for basketball, not egg-eating ability. Judging from their size, it looked as though the Lake Placid boys made a run-away of it. The two Stevens boys, who were later to win the Olympic bob-sled championship, could doubtless eat almost a crate of eggs between them. The other three Lake Placid boys looked almost as capable.

Each team took its place on the floor. Mrs. Stevens came in with a large pan of hard-boiled eggs. Mr. Stevens announced that the scoring would be the same as in basketball—except no fouls. Nobody was allowed to wash down his eggs with anything. Referee Stevens blew the whistle. We started. The Lake Placid boys stuffed in twenty eggs. The Herkimer boys stuffed in twenty-two eggs. Little Ed Murnane ate six.

Herkimer had won its second contest of the evening. Soon everyone went to bed, but Eddie didn't stay in bed long, because the eggs wouldn't stay in Eddie. So the team didn't leave Lake Placid as early as we had expected the next day.

When our train pulled into Herkimer and we all piled out and tramped home, there was Papa at the front gate with a broom handle, ready to give me the beating of my life. However, before he could land a blow, I pulled out my $300 and waved it in front of him. That was more than he had made in a whole year at Diemel and Snell's Lumber Yard. Or at the store in two months. I had earned it in a week! The broom handle was lowered. I turned the $300 over to my mother. Her $10 investment had paid off 3000 per cent.

In fairness to Papa, I must say that without formal education he made a great success of his business ventures. Neither my father nor my mother ever saw a basketball game, even during the later years when most of my time was spent promoting basketball. They couldn't understand how I could go to school and promote basketball. Neither did I. My father was convinced that all I "took up" in school was "time" and that my best subject was "recess." I stayed in the sixth grade until I was able to vote for President. My seat was never removed until the day North School was torn down. Then I decided I'd had enough and quit.

In 1904 I had an entirely different team. The players of the year before wanted $8 a game. That was too much. The new gang agreed to work for $3 per game plus expenses. They were known as the "Celtics" of Utica and were one of the best teams in the state.

The towns we hit were the same—Lake Placid, Tupper Lake, Saranac Lake, Fort Covington, Malone, and Ogdensburg. This time we played two games at Tupper Lake.

The boys' expenses included sleeping quarters and eats. They did their own laundry in hotel wash basins. The year before I had had to pay for the team's laundry. They wouldn't wash it themselves.

Long, lean John Roberts was on the team. John was 6 feet 2—unusually tall for those days. He got his training from "Sid" Clemons, a Utica barber who knew his basketball. John was too modest and polite for basketball in those days. He hated to hurt the smaller fellows who got in his way, but he was a great shot. He would be a star today.

Johnny Wood and Clint Howe were probably the most rugged guards in basketball at the time. Forwards they met found out that Johnny and Clint never stopped to apologize when they went down the floor. John Roberts always apologized if he banged into someone.

Harry Fox, Mike Brothers, and Bradley Hall—the others on that year's team—got their basketball training much as I did, in a cow barn on the Hall farm. They had little schooling and never had a chance to play on a high school team. Hall later played with Utica in the State League and also with Herkimer.

As the first Celtic team in the country, we defeated the New York 23rd Street YMCA at Saranac Lake in 1905.

Johnny Wood and Clint Howe played the violin. Harry Fox was a good singer. So we decided to add an act to our basketball exhibition. I got a little extra guarantee for a special attraction we thought up. Since Bradley Hall was a better athlete than actor, he sat in the audience and applauded.

At Tupper Lake we put forth our wares after beating them two games, 24–20 and 19–15. Wood and Howe borrowed violins from the orchestra that was to play for the dancing. After a few twists on the strings, they were ready. They played and we all sang "The Old Oaken Bucket." The audience, led by Bradley Hall, clapped loudly. Anyway, at the dance, I got the pick of the girls.

After the game we went back to our hotel. There was a lot of excitement. We were heroes. Many offered to buy us drinks. But the boys refused. Soon the crowd went away and the boys went off to bed.

After everything had quieted down in the lobby, I set myself the job of figuring up my finances. I didn't have any paper handy, so I used some lying on the clerk's desk. After a great deal of figuring, I was satisfied that I was in the "black." I crumpled up the paper and threw it into the wastebasket. Then I went to bed.

All the guests, including ourselves, slept soundly. Nothing disturbed us—not even the daily 6 A.M. train, although its whistle blew and blew. It wasn't until around 10 o'clock that anyone discovered something was wrong. Then it seemed that all the sleepers woke at once. People quickly checked their watches. Ten o'clock! They dashed downstairs to check the clock in the hotel lobby. Ten o'clock! They began calling loudly for the hotel keeper. He, too, was still in bed. He sat up and looked at his watch. Ten o'clock!

"Why wasn't I called?" demanded first one irate guest, then another. The poor man was stupified.

"No one left any calls last night," he said.

"We did, we did," they yelled. They had left calls for the 6-o'clock train. It was the only train leaving Tupper Lake until 4:30 that afternoon.

The baggage man at the station had called to find out where all the guests were who usually rushed in at the last minute to hop on the train. The engineer had tooted his whistle several times to hurry up the crowd. No explanation was offered.

Harry Fox and I awoke about 10, too. No one could sleep with all the racket going on in the lobby. Fox looked at his watch. Ten o'clock!

"Hey," he yelled, "it's 10 o'clock." He ran around trying to dress and wake the other boys at the same time. We were supposed to have made the 6-o'clock train. Together we raced downstairs and joined the angry crowd of late-sleepers. The poor clerk insisted no one had signed the call sheet. All of us in turn insisted we had.

Someone suggested looking through the wastepaper basket. The lost call sheet was found, crumpled, twisted, and with figures scrawled all over its back. I never admitted my guilt. I don't think I'd be writing this book if I had. The angry crowd went off to the dining room to eat. So did we. Someone said he hoped the guy who pulled that trick would choke. I almost did.

A wonderful example of the basketball teams produced nearly fifty years ago in the Mohawk Valley was the 1902–03 and 1903–04 team that took the floor for Little Falls High School. For two years this quintet never met defeat at the hands of a high school team. So superior were they to teams of their own age that they finally were compelled to play professional and college teams.

Among the professional teams were the famed Twenty-third Streets of New York, the Knickerbockers of New York, the Crescents of Patterson, N. J., the All-Troy team of Troy, Company E of Schenectady, the Cortland Athletics of Cortland, N. Y., the Pastimes of Syracuse, the Buffalo Germans, and the Deaf Mutes of New York.

Among the colleges were Syracuse U., Colgate, Potsdam Normal, St. Lawrence, Union, and Hamilton College.

I recall one interesting series the Little Falls basketeers played. Shortly after Company E of Schenectady journeyed to Kansas City in 1904 and nailed the World's AAU Championship, the Little Falls team challenged them to a series. They reluctantly agreed.

In the first game, played in Schenectady, Company E won. The following week the two teams met in Little Falls with the home team winning. It was decided to play the rubber game on a neutral court, and Amsterdam was selected because it was the nearest point midway between the two cities.

At the game-ending whistle the score was all tied up at 25–all. At the beginning of the overtime period the Electric City team jumped into the lead on a foul throw. With the seconds sliding away, Bert Schell, Little Falls forward, threw a desperation pass the length of the court hoping it would fall into the right hands. Schell, in order to pass over the hands of the opposition, arched the ball—but too much. It hit the wall and spiraled through the hoop. Little Falls had won, 27–26.

The next year I had a team which included Eddie Kern and Jim Murnane from Herkimer, Irving Leon and Stauring Walrath from Little Falls, and myself. On Thanksgiving of 1905, as we were taking the same trip through the north country, Leon and Walrath told me they had to go to Watertown. They wanted to visit two girls who had moved there from Little Falls. They agreed to meet the team at Alexandria Bay where we were supposed to play. But the two never showed up.

Jim and I waited at the hall until 9 P.M., but still no Leon and Walrath. I tried to explain to the local manager, who ran a laundry, that the two were stranded in Watertown. I suggested he loan us a couple of his players. I even suggested using two volunteers from the crowd just so we could play and get our $60 guarantee. He said no. He was furious.

The crowd of seven hundred was impatient for action; so the manager hastily gathered his committee together and they decided to give the crowd their money back. We lost $60. I was broke. I told Murnane and Kern to get in the line to the cashiers' windows and try to collect a 50¢ refund apiece. They did. It was the only money we had.

We were very hungry. We asked the manager if he would at least give us a dinner and car fare to Redwood, our next stop. But he wouldn't. We asked him about a place to sleep and he suggested we try the river.

Broke, tired, and hungry in a strange town, we trudged off down the street. We went in the first hotel we came to and found there a kind woman who listened to our story. She agreed to put us up for the night and also insisted we have something hot to eat. That was the closest we came to a Thanksgiving dinner that year.

None of us slept very well. Three big boys in one bed is too many. Besides, the springs kept sticking up through the thin mattress every time someone changed position.

I helped Murnane and Kern eat up their $1.00 for breakfast. Then we took the horse car for Redwood, hoping that we could beg the conductor of the Utica train for a lift. As we boarded the horse car, the conductor asked for fares. They amounted to 60¢ for the three of us. But it might as well have been $60. All we had was 10¢.

Kern, a doctor's son, had a watch his grandfather had left him. It was on a long brass chain. Murnane offered to put the watch up as collateral. Kern was unhappy. "Grandpa would turn over in his grave if I done that," he wailed.

Murnane reassured him. "Don't worry about Grandpa, they probably buried him on his stomach anyway." The conductor let us ride free to Redwood.

Murnane, Kern, and myself hung around the Redwood railroad station hoping some miracle would get us home. Two women came in. When they learned from the ticket agent that their train was two hours late, they sat down and unpacked a lunch. First cheese, then crackers, bread, and a piece of home-made cake.

Three mouths were watering all the time. Finally I got

up my courage and asked the ladies if the cheese was made locally.

"Oh, yes," they said, "only a mile down the road. Would you like to try some?"

We sure would! The two women had almost five pounds with them. When we three got through, they had barely a quarter-pound. But they didn't care. We finished off the crackers, too. They ate the cake themselves.

When the train for Utica finally came, we thanked the ladies and jumped on—just as though we had money for fares. Then we all slid way down in our seats, hoping no one would take notice. But the conductor didn't miss a thing. In fact, the conductor was Harry Crandall from Herkimer. He knew us and you would have thought he was president of the railroad the way he arranged our passage to Utica with transfers to Herkimer.

The northern tours were so successful that when the next year (1906) came around, I undertook to manage still another team. This time it was the well-known 31st Separate Company of Herkimer, the grand-daddy of champions. I took over the Mohawk Armory and played several home games before starting out on the road. Travel was inviting for many reasons, most of all because it was more profitable.

In North Adams, Mass., that year, we played Eddie Long's famous North Adams Stars and won 38–31. We felt sure then we could take on the best the country had to offer. In our next two games we did just that. The teams were Brattleboro and St. Johnsbury, Vermont.

Basketball in Vermont prior to 1900 was dominated by the Brattleboro Athletics and Co. D of St. Johnsbury. They battled annually for the state championship and Brattleboro always won. Not until 1905–6 did professionals start playing on these teams. Until then, they had been made up of home talent. With the coming of the pros, Brattleboro and St. Johnsbury ranked with the best teams in the country.

Ed Wachter of Troy came with his brother Lew to play with Brattleboro. Others were Jimmy Williamson, Jim Davey, Flo Haggerty, Bill Hardiman, Ed Doran, and Chief Muller.

On the St. Johnsbury team were Toby Mathews (who invented the one-hand shot so popular these days), Jimmy Doyle, Harry Henshel, Bob Swenson, Eddie Hollenbeck, Paul Steinberg, Jack Fox, Bill Corbett, and Eddie Vaughn.

In going from North Adams to St. Johnsbury to play, I got my distances and directions mixed up. We made a long detour. I spent nearly all of the money I'd made thus far on useless train fare. By the time we got to St. Johnsbury, I was broke. It was very early in the morning. This is what I wrote my mother about our near-disaster:

Dear Mother:

When Columbus discovered this beautiful country of ours, I know it was impossible for him to go through any more hardship than my team and I went through getting to St. Johnsbury.

It is easy to appreciate what miracle Columbus performed when he discovered America, but it looked like he left St. Johnsbury for me. If he did, after all the hardship we certainly landed in a real place for friendship.

I am sure that before I ever start out trying to explore any more towns, I will first find out the difference between one mile and three miles, because with the guarantee I am getting for playing here, the arithmetic that I am using will perform miracles of faith, but it will drive me right back into the sixth grade in school. I know my teacher would rather see the school burn down than have me come back.

Last night we played in N. Adams, Mass., a nice place and a long way from home. The only trouble there was that Eddie Long, the manager, wrote me in a letter that he couldn't pay much because they don't draw. But you should see the packed house. I was only getting $50, so I held him up and got $15 more. When I say I held him up I don't mean he was fainting. That's what they call a miracle of Charity instead of a miracle of Faith.

The mistake I made before I left was that I should have bought a share in the railroad company. At 4 in the morning while the roosters were crowing and the cows were getting ready to give their morning milk, we arrived at the railroad station here in St. Johnsbury, Vt., with but a few nickels among us. The trouble was that I gave the boys money to send home souvenirs to their mothers and I had just enough to get here.

Along came a beautiful milk wagon. I gave the horse pulling the wagon the sign to stop. The milkman thought we were a bunch of bandits. We certainly looked the part. We told him we were basketball players. He gave us all a bottle of milk. We offered to pay him but he refused and said it was on him. Just to leave the empty bottles in the baggage room at the railroad station where we were stopping.

I am writing this letter on this railroad paper in the station and it's 5:30 A.M. The boys are all stretched out on the hard benches trying to get a little rest.

I will write you all about this trip. I am just going to take a snooze and the good baggage man is putting mail bags under the boys heads and covering them up with burlap bags. When I told the man we were basketball players, he realized we needed rest and called the hotel proprietor. A bus with a nice pair of horses picked us up and took us all to the hotel. The hotel proprietor made us all go to bed.

We woke up at noon and the proprietor with nice plump cheeks as red as roses and a front like a pregnant woman said, "Boys have dinner with me." What a feed! Ham and eggs with real German Fried potatoes, home-made bread, apple pie, and more good milk. I didn't eat the ham. I had four fried eggs in butter. Oh, yes, Mother, he gave us some Herkimer County cheese and asked us if this would make us homesick.

At about 5 P.M. we wandered over to the post office. The proprietor insisted we return for supper. The post office had the best crowd of any other business place. We hung around the post office a while and read the mail that had been discarded by the business men of the village. After reading the mail, we moved to the hotel where supper was waiting.

The way this hotel proprietor took care of us, you would think he had money on us to beat the local team. After feeding us he made us take a good rest before going over to the armory. We stayed all night and had breakfast and he wouldn't take a cent, which was at least a saving of about $12. And you noticed I used his paper and envelopes to finish this letter.

– – – – T I M E – – – –

I didn't finish the letter. I wanted to see what happened in Brattleboro. We lost in St. Johnsbury and also in Brattleboro, but no disgrace, Mother. We played the best teams in the country. I told the boys to write home and ask their mothers to pray for these people in St. Johnsbury and Brattleboro. I will tell you all about it when I get home. With the savings I had from the hotel and milkman and if I get home without any trouble I should have $40 left after I pay the boys. This will leave me about $200 for the year. Mother, dear, when you light the candles Friday night, please say a prayer for Fred Knowlton, the milkman, and his family and his cows; for the baggage man, Frank Blossom, and his family; and that fine hotel man, Herbert Moore, and his family. God bless them all!

Back home again. But I couldn't stay idle. I scheduled more games right away. In fact, I scheduled two games for the same night in February, 1906—one in Watertown and one in Cortland.

I had only five men on my team. Not an easy number to split. Managers of both the Watertown and Cortland teams insisted I keep my agreements. It would be bad policy to cancel either game. Schedules in the future might suffer.

I finally decided to send my regular team on to Watertown while I tried to round up another team for the Cortland game. Then I learned that two of my regulars, the Bradshaw twins from Schenectady, had the mumps. That eliminated them from the Watertown game. So I now had to find seven, not five players.

I called on Irving Leon and Stauring Walrath of Little Falls, veterans of another northern tour. They agreed to play in the Watertown game. That was one hurdle. But it was the morning before the Cortland game and I still had to assemble another complete team to play in Cortland by nightfall.

In desperation I went to Utica to see if Sol Goldbas, an outstanding athlete, could help me out. When I told him my dilemma, he immediately came up with a suggestion. "Let's go to Syracuse," he said. So we did, on the next street car. It was 3 P.M. when we arrived at the University. Lucky for us, the school's players were practicing in the gym. Goldbas called one of them over.

"How would you like to make five bucks?" he asked.

"Doing what?" the player demanded.

"Playing basketball at Cortland tonight," came the answer.

"O.K." Just like that.

Goldbas asked, "Can you get two more players to go?"

"Yes, for $5."

Three University stars, Goldbas, and myself were on the 5:45 train for Cortland. The players used assumed names. Playing for money would kill their amateur standing. I purchased five white jerseys so the group would look like an A-1 ball club. We took the Cortland team easily. My regulars in Watertown also won. Two victories, two purses, huge success—so I thought.

But misfortune closed in. Someone had recognized the University lads. It was reported to the Syracuse coach. He disqualified them from further play with their school team. He also sent for me.

"Young man," he said, when I entered his office, "do you realize these boys have lost their amateur standing by accepting your money?"

"I'm sorry, really I am," I said. "If receiving the money harms their standing, I will be glad to take back the $5 I paid each of them. You have my consent to return their amateur standing to them."

So glib was I!

Something in his tone, something in his look, made me change tactics immediately. The coach was dead-serious. This was no laughing matter to him. I offered the best apology I could think of at the moment. I even went further. I promised that, if the incident were forgotten, when I married and had children I would send them to Syracuse. (And I did, too—Leatrice, Eleanor, Irving, and Sheldon!)

As I was about to leave, the coach assured me the boys would be reinstated. I asked him what would happen to the $15 I'd paid them. The coach replied, "It will be difficult to find the leakage."

"But how can they be reinstated and keep my money?" I said.

"Faith, hope, and charity," he answered.

That was the last time I ever asked college kids with amateur standings to play on one of my teams.

When I arrived home and opened my mail, I found a pleasant surprise: an offer of $35 to bring my team to Syracuse to play the Pastime Five. They must have heard how we beat Cortland and Watertown in one day. Naturally, I accepted the offer.

In preparation for the Pastime game, I picked one star from Utica, Jim Conway, for $3 and expenses, and three other players at $2 and expenses.

I had never heard of the Pastimes. I thought they probably were a bunch of kids around eighteen or nineteen years old. It was quite a shock to walk out on that floor and find players anywhere from seven to eight years older than we were.

I must confess that when I started this book, I did not plan to mention this game—simply because I had conveniently forgotten all about it. But last year, when my son Shelly and I were looking through some old Syracuse *Herald Journal* newspapers, Shelly came to the February 2, 1906, issue. He turned to the sport page. There it was: PASTIMES DEFEAT HERKIMER 102–10.

"Father, dear," Shelly said in a mock innocent tone of voice, "do you remember the name of the man you played against forty-four years ago?" (You see, I have never been able to convince my sons Shelly and Irving that I was a better basketball player than they.)

"Yes, I remember," I said uneasily. "It was Eddie Dorner."

"Look, Father, dear," Shelly continued, "Mr. Dorner got 33 baskets. That's 66 points."

"Yes," I agreed, "33 baskets certainly make 66 points." I had a premonition something was coming.

"And do you remember, Father, dear, that you made only one basket?" Shelly said, gloating.

"Honest, Shelly, I'll be darned. I'd forgotten all about this," I said.

"Hey, Dad, what are you blushing for?" he said.

I closed the book quickly.

It was Saturday, the first week in March, 1906. I was eighteen years old and I knew I never would get to Harvard College. I had been successful as a Globe Trotter for nearly three years, and now I very much wanted to try my luck at promoting a basketball game. So I went to Dad to get a small loan from the funds which I had made on my barnstorming trips in the past three years and which I had turned over to him.

Standing beside his old roll top desk while I was looking out of the window watching the falling snow, Dad lowered his 240 pounds into his swivel chair and, just as if he were a banker, refused to make me the loan. It was an unexpected turndown. My anger produced butterflies in my stomach, but I was more than ever determined to show my father I could make good.

I accomplished my goal by hard work. As the site for my first venture as a promoter, I chose Richfield Springs, about seventeen miles from Herkimer. In the early part of 1906 I had played for the Richfield team against Oneonta and had practically won the game single-handed by scoring every one of Richfield's 23 points. Naturally, I became a hero to Richfield fans, especially to the young girls who gathered at the home of Police Chief Stitts. His daughter, incidentally, was kind of sweet on me.

Richfield was a beautiful summer resort known for its sulphur baths and its beautiful hotels. At that time the population was about 10,000 in the summer and 3500 in the winter.

I secured the Masonic Hall, the only building in Richfield where a basketball game could be played, and then hired the Richfield town basketball team for $5 and gave my Herkimer team the same amount. For another $5 I engaged a five-piece orchestra from Herkimer to play at the dance after the game, and as an added attraction I engaged two wrestlers to give an exhibition between the halves.

It was Saturday and the folks from the Mohawk Valley could stay up late. I had chartered a special trolley car for $20 to take sixty people to Richfield and back. Now, my job was to get people talking about the gala evening. I sold fifty tickets at 75¢ each. These entitled the purchaser to the trolley ride, the game, the dance, and the wrestling.

I wanted to show my home town that the name of Basloe was magic. The night of the game, my chartered trolley car was packed with sixty people, and there were more who wanted to go.

I had to promise the parents of my patrons that the lights in my special car would not be turned off. It was a cold night and we sang the latest songs on the long slow trip. When we disembarked a half-hour late, Richfield Springs was deserted. Not a sleigh or cutter was on the road. The temperature was below zero and the snow was deep. It was as though our noisy crowd had arrived in a ghost town. But when we stormed into the hall—orchestra, basketball team, two wrestlers, and our rooters—the place was packed. It was a beautiful discovery for a boy-promoter. The only way I could get the crowd I brought with me in was to shorten up the basketball playing court and have them sit on the floor around the court. I was flushed with pride and joy and sure that everything would come off successfully. I could imagine what people would say about my promotional talents.

After the first half of the game, I announced to the folks that the wrestling match was next on the program, but to my chagrin only one of the wrestlers, Fat Munson, appeared. Flat-Foot Barber was nowhere to be found. I asked if anyone in the audience would wrestle Fat Munson. Nobody offered to. I had to make this first plunge a sensational success; so I decided to take on Munson myself, even though I had just played twenty minutes of rough, hard basketball. Weighing only 145 to Munson's 220, I knew I'd be murdered; but the show just had to be a hit.

As I came out, the huge pair of trunks I had borrowed from Munson showed signs of the state of my morale. The crowd roared. With my big flat feet, I was a caricature of a wrestler. It was doubly humiliating to know that my girl was watching. We shook hands. Munson immediately lifted me up to his belly button and dropped me to the floor for a big laugh. Then the big tub of lard fell on me and began to crush the life out of me, but he couldn't pin my shoulders to the mat because I was round-shouldered. I did all I could to help him pin my shoulders but they wouldn't touch the mat at the same time. So there I stayed, on my back squirming like a snake, groaning and grunting and begging Fat Munson to get off. I grew madder with every thump he gave me. "You darn fool! Let me up!" I kept yelling. In my rage I pinched his rump as hard as I could. "Get off me, you big tub of lard!" Earl Jones, the referee, finally called the match a draw and probably saved my life.

I had made all our team's points in the first half of the basketball game and I saw a chance to save face in the eyes of my girl and the crowd. I told my teammates to feed me the ball. I had to be a hero in Richfield Springs. We won 18–12, and I made all 18 points. Dancing followed and everybody had a swell time.

We got back to Herkimer early Sunday morning. All the rest of the kids went to Nagle's Beanery for breakfast, but I went home to wake up Mother and show her my earnings as a promoter. Mother was awake waiting for me to come home. On the big kitchen table I spread out the green cabbage and silverware. When it was all counted and my bills deducted, I had $102.50 left for myself.

When I finished with a glass of milk and some bread and butter, I lifted Mother onto my lap, gave her a big hug and kiss, and then piled into bed, a mighty proud and happy kid.

The Mohawk Valley League was organized in 1906. It included Johnstown, Canajoharie, Fort Plain, Herkimer, Frankfort, Gloversville, Little Falls, and Utica. It developed some of the fastest basketball in the country and was a financial success. Our 31st of Herkimer won the championship in 1906–7 and 1907–8.

That last season, Fort Plain featured one of the first Negroes ever to play professional basketball. His name was Frank (Dido) Wilson. Frank was offered many contracts with other teams, but he preferred to stay around home with his brother Bidey who was a baseball player. Frank was also an excellent baseball player.

With my 1907–8 team of Jim Murnane, Min Bradshaw, Mike Roberts, Mike Brothers, and Blubs Alberding. I decided to go south to New York and then swing around through New England. We took on the 4th Separate Company of Yonkers, N. Y., and won 28–26. Then we boarded the overnight boat from New York to Boston.

In the morning I got up early and went down to the dining room. I hoped I could eat my breakfast and then sneak back to my cabin before the rest of the gang woke up. I ordered oatmeal, two eggs, pancakes, toast, and coffee—a big breakfast for me. Ordinarily a 25¢ meal was enough for me.

I had just started eating when the whole bunch came in. The salt air gave them big appetites. They grabbed up the menus, took a good look at the pile on my plate, and began ordering everything they could think of—grapenuts with cream, eggs, ham, bacon, buckwheat cakes, syrup, coffee, and toast. Everyone had two portions. To top it all off, they ordered cooked pears. I loved cooked pears, but I had decided I couldn't afford them. So I sat and watched those bums gobble them down by the dish. I vowed that when we got to Boston one plate of baked beans was all they'd get. After I paid the $8.20 meal ticket, I barely had enough carfare to get to Providence, where our next game was scheduled. Here's a letter I wrote from Providence to my mother.

Dear Mother:

I don't suppose you ever heard of Providence, Rhode Island. I never dreamed I would ever come here where Brown University is located. For the real winter weather we are having this year it is rather mild here. Many of the college boys are going without overcoats. I know we're glad we have ours. They have caps that fit on the back of their heads. It looks like the capmakers ran out of material when they made those college caps. They wear no rubbers—no wonder mothers worry when the boys are away from home. The team and myself must be a bunch of sissies. Providence is nothing like I expected it to be except for a college city. I expected to see an old town with buildings as old as Washington, but instead they're very nice. They have excellent streets, fine stores, and everybody looks prosperous here but me. We got a good workout tonight, which is Friday, by playing a pick-up college star team called the All-States Stars. If this team had been together before, the score might have been just in the reverse instead of 27–19 in our favor. They had some good players, especially one boy by the name of George Haggerty who will be a great star some day. They tell me he comes from Springfield, Mass.

I had a great experience here, Mother. The boys certainly put one over on your son, Frankie. I watched these college boys on the Main Square at about 11:15 P.M. last night all flocking to one big restaurant which is near the University. I said to the boys on my team that this restaurant is sure very popular with the big crowds all marching to this one place. So the Murnane boy said, "Frank, the reason the crowds all go to this place is that every Friday night this particular restaurant gives away free eats between 11 and 12 o'clock." I fell for this as easily as Manila fell for Admiral Dewey.

I said, "Boys, let's go! What are we waiting for?"

On all other occasions the evening snack is always "pay your own." So we all entered the overcrowded restaurant and parked way in the rear where the doors to the kitchen swing in and out, just missing our table. The noise of the tools and the dishes drowned out all conversation. Immediately we were confronted by a lovely blonde waitress who had been deserted by her husband. He must be a "dirty rat" to desert such a nice girl. She looked as though she would give birth at any time. We visited with her. She had a Scotch brogue. She asked us where we were from and we told her Herkimer, New York. She wanted to know if we knew Chester Gillette, the boy that was accused of murdering Grace Brown in the Big Moose up in the Adirondacks. I wonder why she asked us this question? I wonder if she had anything on her mind?

After we got through eating, and the conversation was at an end, she handed a piece of paper to Murnane. I thought he was dating up a pregnant woman. He got chummy and left her fifty cents on the table as we all started to walk out. As we approached the exit door, the cashier asked, "Who has the check?"

"What check?" was my reply.

"For the eats."

The players kept going and left me alone with the cashier who was built like a wrestler. All he wanted from me was $6.90.

"I thought everybody ate all they wanted without paying between the hours of 11 and 12."

"Look," he said, "my boss pays rent between the hours of 11 and 12. He also pays for the food and the help between 11 and 12. Kick in with the $6.90 or I'll take it out of your hide."

The team was outside looking in the front window laughing while I was suffering and the customers who were still eating were getting a big laugh at my expense. Well, Mother, dear, your boy Frankie paid, which proves you don't get anything for nothing. I suppose one has to live and learn. At least, I will never forget Providence, R.I., the restaurant, and the pregnant waitress.

With love,
Frank

We arrived in Gloucester just in time to see the famous Fish Hatchery fire. The game was delayed for several hours that evening while the local volunteers battled the flames. The game, once it got started, was a ball of fire itself. Stuffy McInnis of baseball fame played for Gloucester.

He was an artist at using his hips and elbows. I played for ten minutes against him. I was glad it was only ten minutes. After forty minutes, they had beaten us 32–30.

That summer I gave up basketball—temporarily. I wanted to go on the stage. The stunts that my teams and I had put on after the games up north spurred me to try my hand at professional vaudeville. I got together Jack Pryor, Mike Brothers, and Harry Fox. We became known as "The Grant Comedy Four." Our act had its first professional opening in Rome, N. Y., in May, 1908. It was an immediate success.

We featured a "School Day" skit. We wrote our own jokes and words and music for the songs. On many occasions along the Keith Circuit, we appeared on the same program with W. C. Fields, Buster Keaton, James Barton, Chick Sales, and the Dolly Sisters.

But the act lasted only a year. In June, 1909, we returned to Herkimer from a swing through the circuit. Harry Fox went off to Richfield Springs for a holiday. It was his last. He was drowned. We were so broken up over his death that we never went back on the stage again. Nobody could take Harry Fox's place. I went to work for my father.

In 1909 I again organized the 31st and signed up Howard Bradshaw, Jack Andre of Frankfort, Brad Hall and James Conway of Utica, and Murnane of Herkimer. The next year this team, one of the best I ever managed, defeated the world-famous Buffalo Germans before 2800 people in the Mohawk Armory. But things were happening elsewhere in basketball. Until that game, the Germans had won 110 straight games.

CHAPTER SIX

AN UNRULY BEAR CUB

BASKETBALL proved to be an unruly bear cub in the family of sports. Intended only as "milk recreation," a sport for YMCA boys during the long cold winters, it leaped suddenly to popularity. It became fast-moving, scientific, strenuous.

At first, you'll recall, there were no rules. Only general "instructions." Lambert Will devised most of the "rules" in Herkimer. Other towns made up their own rules. In Trenton, N. J., for example, teams were made up of nine men. They were all rovers. That is, they could go at will anywhere on the court. That meant eighteen men scrimmaging for the ball—more like football than modern basketball. In those days everyone followed the ball. There were no zones, no man-to-man defenses. Everyone piled in after the ball, no holds barred.

Systematic playing was impossible. Something had to be done. The first solution was to divide the court into three sections—like the lacrosse playing area. One section was reserved for the forwards, one section for the centers, and the remaining section for the guards. Under this ruling, it was a foul for any player to step out of his zone. The zones were marked by lines painted on the floor.

Referee

Umpire for Kensington

Umpire for Trenton

Time Keeper

Secretary

Length of Halves

TRENTON	Position	Goals from Field	Goals from Fouls	Fouls
1 Stratton	Attack			
2 Bratton	"			
3 Cooper, Capt.	"			
4 Cook	Centre			
5 W. Clayton	"			
6 Buckley	"			
7 S. Clayton	Defence			
8 Bates	"			
9 Harrison	"			
Totals,				

KENSINGTON	Position	Goals from Field	Goals from Fouls	Fouls
1 West, Capt.	Attack			
2 Ebelhare	"			
3 Erskine	"			
4 Burk,	Centre			
5 Page	"			
6 Hessler,	"			
7 Kennedy	Defence			
8 Totten,	"			
9 White	"			
Totals,				

This is the first printed score sheet ever used. Note that the teams had nine players. The teams in and around Herkimer were using only five men as early as 1895. Field goals counted three points; free throws, one. The score was Trenton, 14, Kensington, Pa., 10.

But this system didn't last for long. Soon it was abandoned and all eighteen men piled in after the ball again. Obviously this free-for-all scramble could not develop into a fast, skilled, scientific game. It had to have sensible and universally accepted rules. Lambert Will had discovered this very early in Herkimer. Other towns didn't see it so quickly.

In 1893 in Trenton, where great things were to happen in basketball, two soccer players, Al Bratton and Fred Cooper, turned to basketball. With them came team play and system. Being excellent soccer players, they instantly realized that the passing of soccer could be adapted to basketball. In soccer, passwork was with the feet. In basketball, it would be with the hands.

Cooper and Bratton instituted the passing game in the old Trenton Y. At first, passing was confined to them. But as time went on, the other players became adept at snapping the ball back and forth. There was less confusion, there was more speed, there was better basketball. Passing is what gave Trenton champion teams.

Of course, other teams "passed" the ball. But Trenton had something more than just throwing the ball around. The Trenton system of passing was definite. Its objective was to carry the ball right up to the opponent's basket. A favorite trick of Cooper and Bratton was to pass the ball between them—no one else touching it—from one end of the court to the other.

With this development, basketball was rescued from its chaotic pell-mell scrimmages. It took on a system even while nine-man teams were the rule.

At the close of the 1893–94 season, the undefeated Trenton team was acknowledged to be one of the champion teams of the country. They beat the 23rd St. YMCA of New York City, which in turn had beaten everything in

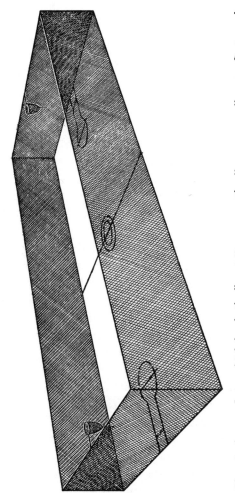

The steel cage from which basketball got its name—the "cage game"—was first used in Bristol, Pa., in 1894. It was designed by Fred Cooper, Al Bratton, and Fred Paderatz, the carpenter who made the first real cage from chicken wire in 1893.

New York and New England. Trenton also cleaned up everything around Philadelphia and New Jersey. Their toughest opponent was a team from Nanticoke, Pa. It took two games to reach a decision, but Trenton finally won.

Other stars on the Trenton team besides Bratton and Cooper were W. J. "Prof" Davison, "Pop" Brower, Sidney Smith, Harry Bates, Charles Hodge, and William Fenton.

The Trenton team played in "Romeo" uniforms—long tights, velvet trunks, and combing stocking pants invented by Fred Cooper. It was also the first team to use glass backboards. In the early 1900's when the team was playing on the stage of the old Masonic Hall, bleachers were placed behind the backboards. In order that the fans on these bleachers could see the games, the management hit upon the idea of using glass for the backboards.

However, the most famous basketball "invention" to come out of Trenton was the "cage game." It came about like this: A reporter of the *True American, State Gazette,* and *Trenton Times* was watching the Trenton team work out one day. Peter Wurflein remarked that they looked lie a lot of monkeys and should be put in a cage. Instead of being insulted, Fred Paderatz, manager of the team, thought there might be a practical idea in the wisecrack.

Fred was not only manager of the team but also a carpenter by trade. He built a chicken-wire cage for the basketball court, leaving holes for four entrances. The cage was eight feet high. Play in this cage was much, much faster. There was no such thing as an out-of-bounds ball. From the opening whistle, play continued without interruption. Basketball instantly picked up speed. It wasn't long before the team of Cooper and Bratton improved on the original chicken-wire fence idea by building a more durable steel mesh cage.

A man was placed at each end of the cage on the out-

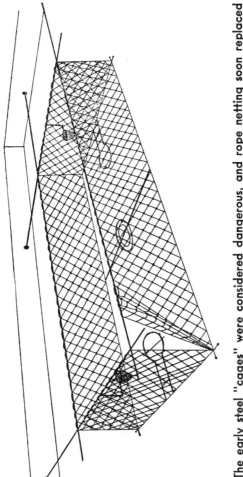

The early steel "cages" were considered dangerous, and rope netting soon replaced them. In the early days of the 20th century the famed Wachter Brothers, Troy, N.Y., made a number of improvements in the "rope" courts.

side to return the ball to play should it be thrown over the cage. These men were members of the team and would alternate positions during the game.

The Bristol, Pa., team used a rope net for a cage. This type of cage became popular throughout Pennsylvania, New Jersey, and New York. Rope nets were much cheaper than steel ones.

Before the cages were introduced, the rules provided that the last man to touch a ball before it went out-of-bounds was entitled to put it in play again. Naturally, the players rushed at top speed after a misdirected ball, hoping to be the last to touch it before it went out. With this sort of play going on, many a bruised first-row spectator was delighted over the rope net.

The Wachter brothers of Troy introduced the cage to Upstaters in the early 1900's. The net was improved with heavier rope and the height was extended to eighteen feet. This net was in truth a cage. It also did away with the goal tender at each end, since the ball seldom got over an eighteen-foot net.

Although the cage became very popular in the East, only two teams in the West used it—Red Wing, Minn. and Fond du Lac, Wis. In the East the nets were fastened to the floor. In the West they were fastened to a four-foot high wall known as the "fence." The top of the net was reinforced with one-inch pine planking, nailed to the rafters.

Basketball fans today have missed something by not seeing play in a net. If, by some miracle, nets, open baskets, and the center jump after every point were to be brought back, you would see *real* basketball again. The little man would once again have his day in basketball. The modern game, slowed down by too much whistle-blowing and foul-calling and overpopulated with tall, skinny giants, would improve.

The next big change in basketball came with the introduction of the open basket without backboard. This type of basket was closed at the bottom, like the one first used in Herkimer. At first, a broom handle was used to poke the ball out after each goal. Soon Spalding introduced a basket to replace Lambert Will's creation. The Spalding basket also had a closed bottom, but it featured a long chain which released the ball after each score.

Another novel sort of basket was featured at Washington Heights, N. J. There swivel baskets were hung at the end of a six-foot iron rod. Unless the ball fell directly in the net, the rim looped the loop and upset the basket. Skill was at a premium in Washington Heights!

Despite the many improvements Trenton gave basketball, most of the facilities were still crude. The Nanticoke, Pa., team, for instance, played in a hall that was heated by hot steam pipes attached to the walls close to the floor. Players received ugly burns when held, pushed, or dragged against them. At Wilmington, Del., the Trenton squad played on a small floor which was heated by an old-fashioned pot-bellied stove. It was difficult to dodge this red-hot menace. Temple College of Philadelphia presented another type of obstacle course. Their floor was long and narrow with but one basket in view. The other was obscured by a large boiler. In shooting for this goal, the players had to throw the ball over the boiler. A player knew he had scored if the ball did not drop to the floor.

The early game was decidedly a "contact" sport. Referees didn't waste air blowing their whistles every minute. In one Trenton game against Millville, Pa., the referee, one Marvin Riley, Sr., carried a revolver in his back pocket. A Trenton player was knocked cold on the floor and the

The Spalding Regulation Basket Ball

Regulation size, fine leather cover with capped ends. Bladder of selected quality. Complete in box.

No. 16. The Spalding Regulation Basket Ball. Each, **$3.00**

No. 18. Practice Ball, regulation size. Each, **$1.50**

EXTRA BLADDERS

No. 27. For above bags.
Each, **70c.**

Spalding's Official Basket Ball Goals

No. 80.
Per pair, **$3.50**

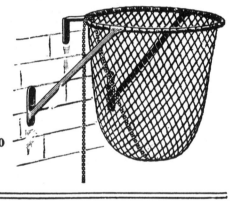

The first regulation basket was used in 1898. Made by Spalding, it had a chain attached to remove the ball from the basket when a goal was scored.

Millville fans proceeded to kick him in the face. He ended up with a broken jaw. Many a time the Trenton fans left Millville after a game under a hail of bricks.

I was just eleven years old when the National Basketball League was organized in the summer of 1898. Probably the first organization of its kind in the United States, the League was created to save basketball from utter confusion and extinction. Up to that time basketball had been a YMCA baby. But it had outgrown the Y. When it proved to be a detriment to their regular physical programs, the majority of Y's dropped the sport. But the players continued, as in Herkimer, to play basketball outside the Y. For a time all went well with these scattered teams. They played rough, personally worked out schedules, manager with manager, town with town.

Then the trouble began. Unscrupulous managers took up the sport as a money-making scheme. The public was treated to a mongrel brand of basketball which did the future of the sport no good. Players appeared on half a dozen teams each season. The team that paid the most drew the best players for that night. Games were cancelled at the last moment and picked teams put on in place of advertised attractions. Good teams were robbed of their just victories by incompetent and biased officials. The established playing rules were disregarded to such an extent that many of the contests degenerated into pure rough and tumble fights. Consequently people began to find other places to spend their money for entertainment. Somehow, this unruly bear cub had to be tamed before it ran completely wild.

The National Basketball League was organized on Dec. 1, 1898, with six clubs—Trenton, Millville, Bicycle Club of Philadelphia, Hancock A. A. of Philadelphia, Germantown of Philadelphia, and Camden, N. J.—and it began the job of cleaning up basketball.

It was not all easy sailing. Before the New Year two of the clubs had dropped out. The four other teams had proved too fast for Hancock and Germantown. Unable to keep up with the others and losing games too often, their attendance fell off at home. That year Trenton won the

George W. Childs cup and the Spalding Pennant after defeating Millville in a vicious free-for-all game 14–7.

Troy, N. Y., was represented in the Hudson River Basketball League from 1909–1911 and in the New York State League from 1911 to 1915. During its seasons in the State League, Troy won four championships and finished second in 1914. The fact that Troy had such a remarkable team, however, brought about its downfall. The next season, 1915, Troy led the State League by such a substantial margin that interest waned and the league was disbanded.

There was so much basketball talent on the team that they did not want to disperse. So decided to "globe trot" a little, as my teams had been doing. After all, I had made money. Troy wanted to do the same. They went as far West as Billings, Montana, playing outstanding professional teams in various states and emerging victorious in all their thirty-eight games. The tour was considered a great accomplishment because they played no push-overs. All the games were played on foreign courts, naturally, under different rule interpretations, and under conditions hostile to visiting teams.

The personnel of the Troy team changed many times. But there were four regulars who made up the excellent core. They were Ed Wachter, Lew Wachter, Jimmy Williamson, and Bill Hardiman. These four had been members of the famous Company E team of Schenectady, N. Y., which had won the "World's Championship" in 1905 in Kansas City by defeating the Blue Diamonds in three straight games at Convention Hall. They had also been teammates on the great Company G team of Gloversville, N. Y., before they became the nucleus of the many championship Troy teams in the Hudson River League. Later Jack Inglis, Chief Muller, Dick Leary, Andy Suils, Flo

Frank J. Basloe

Lambert Will, the Physical Instructor at the Herkimer YMCA, who organized the first basketball team and arranged the first game, played Feb. 7, 1891. He also invented the first basketball rules the same year.

(Below) Herkimer YMCA basketball team, the first to play basketball in the United States, Feb. 7, 1891. *Left to right: First row:* Harter, Peterson, Schmidt; *Second row:* Stanchel, Gray, Steele, Will, Collis; *Back row:* Quackenbush, Swarthout, Warner.

The Herkimer YMCA, where the first basketball game ever played was staged on February 7, 1891.

(Below) This Herkimer team played the first professional basketball game in 1893. *Left to right: First row:* Hiram Harter, Simp Peterson, Harry Stanchel. *Second row:* Fritz Gray, Charles Collis, George Steele, William Schmidt.

The Little Falls Athletics. On Nov. 25, 1894, they played the 31st Separate Co. at the opening of the new armory in Mohawk, N. Y., before 1800 people, an unbelievable throng at the time. *Left to right: Front row:* Matt Kennedy, Alex McCullum, Frank Klock, Mgr., Francis Edick. *Back row:* Frank Ottman, Arthur Cunningham, Frank Moyer.

(Below) The Herkimer High School basketball team was the first organized school team in the country. Their decision to play "for the fun of it and not for money" placed them in the amateur class. *Left to right: Front row:* Roy Waterbury, George J. Sluyter, Edward J. Beckingham, Fritz Gray, Mgr. *Standing:* Glen E. Clark, Lawrence Baker, Leon H. Snyder.

The famous 31st Separate Co. team of Herkimer, N. Y., 1902 New York State Champions. *Left to right: First row:* Tobby Smith, Simp Peterson. *Second row:* Turk Daly, Bill Hartigan, Mgr., String Caswell. *Back row:* George Schoemaker, Tink Metzger.

(Below) The Little Falls Athletics imported the great Jack Fox of New York City and Paul Steinberg of Syracuse, the Syracuse University star. Johnny Stark became the first paid basketball coach at Syracuse University. *Left to right: First row:* George Russ, George O'Brien, Johnny Stark, Ted Rogers. *Second row:* Frank Moyer, Charles Fox, Mgr., Matt Kennedy. *Back row:* Jack Fox, Pet Walsh, Ed Kingsbury, Paul Steinberg.

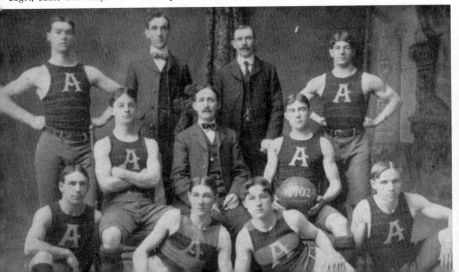

This picture was taken at the age of 16 (1903), when I became the first basketball "globe trotter" and netted myself $300.

(Below) The 31st Separate Co. team of Herkimer. This team, with the exception of Simp Peterson, originally played the preliminary games to the big 31st Separate Co. first team's games, and, with Simp Peterson, in 1903 became the first team. It compiled an outstanding record. *Left to right: First row:* Eddie Murnane, Charlie Greiner. *Second row:* Babe Peterson, Crump Clark, mgr., Jim Murnane. *Standing:* Bert Bowers, Simp Peterson.

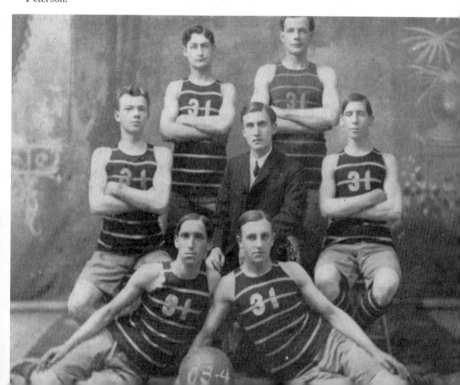

An exact copy of the first basketball program ever printed. The score card is still in excellent condition after 56 years.

The 31st Separate Co. team, champions of the Mohawk Valley Basketball League 1906-07-08-09. *Left to right: Front row:* Mike Brothers, Jim, Murnane, Brad Hall. *Back row:* Minn Bradshaw, Basloe, Hass Bradshaw.

(Below) The Celtics of Utica. This team was organized in 1903 and represented the Basloe Globe Trotters in 1904-05. *Left to right: Front row:* Brad Hall, Johnny Wood, Clint Howe. *Second row:* John Roberts, Sid Clemons. *Standing:* Mike Brothers.

The 31st Separate Co. team that handed the Buffalo Germans their first defeat after a winning streak of 110 straight games. *Left to right: First row:* Big Hass Bradshaw. *Second row:* Bradley Hall, Basloe, Jack Andre. *Back row:* James Murnane, Jim Conway.

(Below) The famous Buffalo Germans, Buffalo, N. Y. This team played 40 minutes of basketball when they averaged 51 years of age, demonstrating their fine conditioning. *Left to right: Standing:* Frederick J. Seames, Supreme President; Edward Miller, guard; Vincent A. Plunkett, Secretary; A. Schell, center; Charles McDonald, president; Albert Post, forward; William Tenjost, treasurer. *Seated:* Henry Faust, guard; W. Rohde, forward; Albert Heerdt, manager; Edward Linneborn, guard; H. Miller, center.

The Little Falls High School team, 1902-03. *Left to right: Front row:* Rollie Gowen, Irv Leon, captain, Clarence Mellor. *Second row:* John Stark, Bert Schell. *Standing:* Harry Leon, Ed Teall, mgr., Harold Smith.

(Below) Fred Cooper, Trenton, N. J., designed this basketball uniform in 1892.

The famous 23rd Street team of New York City was one of the greatest traveling teams of all time. *Left to right: Back row:* Sandy Shields, G. Abadie, Wm. H. Reed, Sr., Grief. *Front row:* Reed, Jr., Wendlekin, R. Abadie.

(Below) Camden, N. J., basketball team, 1898-99, member of the first National Basketball League. *Left to right: Sitting:* Weaver, Zimmerman, Cramer, capt., Ferat, Stewart. *Standing:* Morgenweck, Cartwright, Kelley, Newcomb, Middleton, Austermuhl.

Pennsylvania Bicycle Club basketball team, Philadelphia, 1898-99. *Left to right: Front row:* Price, Rudolph, Carr, Ottey, Heite, Whilt, Hinchliff. *Back row:* Heill, Thomas, McBride, mgr., Woodward, Christensen, Parkhill.

(Below) Bristol, Pa. National League basketball team, 1899. *Left to right: Standing:* Melick, Johnson, Smith, Evernham, Klein. *Sitting:* Crisp, Madeley, Snow, Plant.

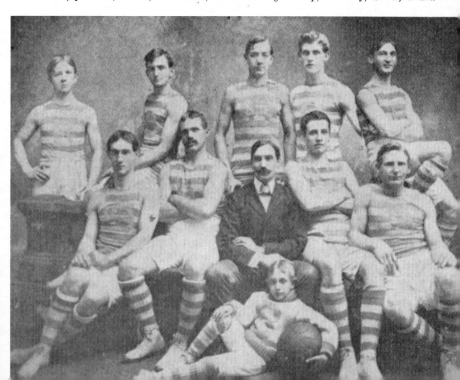

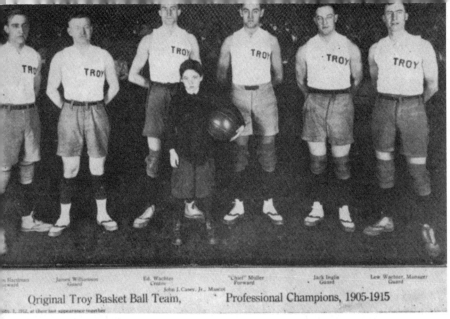

Original Troy Basket Ball Team, Professional Champions, 1905-1915

The famous Troy (N. Y.) team was organized by the Wachter Brothers of Troy.

(Below) 1899 Champion Trenton, N. J., team, members of the first National Basketball League. *Left to right: Standing:* Cooper (coach) Stout, Mascot, A. Cooper, Bratton. *Middle row:* Mellick, Lindsey, Smith (mgr.), Bonham (sec'y), W. Cartlidge. *Front row:* Skin (trainer), Carlidge (capt.), Hamilton, Endebrock, Stinger.

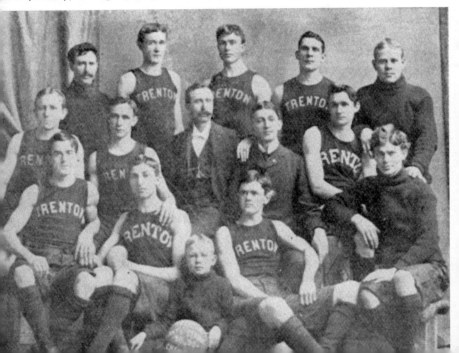

Oswego Indians of 1912-13. During the 1914-15 season this team made one of their greatest tours as the Globe Trotters. Jack LaCasse was replaced by Jack Nolls, the basketball sensation of 1914-15 who was also a great star with Troy. *Left to right:* Basloe, Swede Grimstad, Jack LaCasse, Jim Murnane, Johnny Murphy, Blubs Alberding, Mike Roberts. (Nolls was ill when this picture was taken.)

(Below) This Oswego team defeated the Buffalo Germans three out of four games for the Basketball Championship of the World in 1914 at Buffalo and Oswego. *Left to right:* Basloe, Minn Bradshaw, Wabby Hammond, Jim Murnane, Johnny Murphy, Mike Roberts.

Co. E, Fond du Lac, Wis., United States Basketball Champions, 1898-99. They defeated the Yale University team three straight games at Fond du Lac. *Left to right:* Fog Bartlett, trainer; Brunet, Brunkhorst, Trier, Brugger, mgr.; Bruett (6 ft. 5 in.); Buch, Severin, Rogers, coach; Langlois, timer.

(Below) Co. E team of Fond du Lac, one-time claimants of the World's Basketball Championship. *Left to right: Standing:* Chas. Wright, mgr., Shepard, Choate, Brunkhorst, coach. *Seated:* Fogarty, Longdon, Hawkins, Young, LaPine.

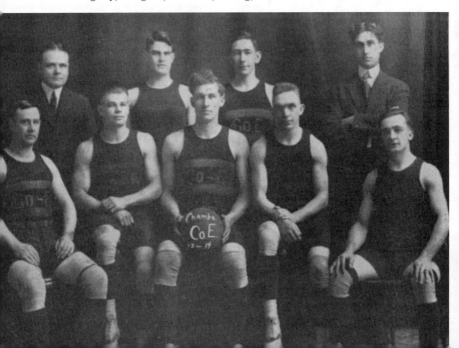

THE HOLD-UP MANAGER

My 1915 open Hudson racer. It cost me $
to overhaul this car before I could use it. *Le*
right: Basloe, Mike Brothers, and Jim Murn

(Left) The basketball management and fan
Fond du Lac, Wis., presented me with this c
boy outfit in 1914. They were sure ano
Jesse James had put in his appearance.

(Below) Clarence Johnson, the first basket
player ever sold by one basketball team to
other. The Basloe Globe Trotters sold hin
Fond du Lac, Wis., in 1917.

F. J. Basloe Is Manager of the Globe
Trotting Basket Ball Team.

Basloe Globe Trotters, formerly the Oswego (N. Y.) Giants, 19195-16. This team represented both the Globe Trotters and Fond du Lac, Wis., by simply turning their jerseys inside out for the customers. *Left to right:* Mike Roberts, Peter LaPine, Johnny Murphy, Basloe, Jim Tormey, and Minn Bradshaw. (Bill Schardt was also a member of this team, but he was at the Brooklyn Dodgers training camp when the picture was taken.)

(Below) The Muscatine, Iowa, team, one of the greatest in the country, had some great baseball stars among its personnel. *Left to right:* D. Sheldon Schuris, Eugene Healy, R. G. Lohr, E. E. Bloom, Jim Cullen, Ed Gould, Bob Hasbrook. *Seated:* George Volger, mgr.

Basloe Globe Trotters 1919-20. These five players completed a 110-game journey. *Left to right:* Basloe, Eddie Murphy, Carl Mariott, Jerk Waters, Bill Dowd, and Chuck Taylor.

(Below) The Basloe Globe Trotters, 1920-21, one of the greatest of all my teams. They won 51 straight games without a defeat, playing 129 games during the season and losing only 5. *Left to right:* Mike Roberts, Shan Kellmurray, Toots McBride, Bill Ladeaseur, Joe Kellmurray, Bill Dowd, Basloe.

The New York Whirlwinds. Those who remember this famous team consider it the greatest ever assembled. The Whirlwinds disbanded in the spring of 1921 after the historic series with the Celtics. Playing before 11,000 fans, they won the first game 40-24; while the Celtics the second game 26-24 before 8000. *Left to right: Seated:* Marty Friedman, Cris Leonard. *Standing:* Barney Sedran, Ray Kennedy, Harry Riconda, Nat Holman.

(Below) Mike Roberts signing his tenth contract with me. He coached the 1920-21 season, his last year as a Globe Trotter. That team played 129 games and won all but five. It won three so-called world championship games that year — against Muscatine, Iowa; Beloit, Wis.; and the New York Nationals.

The famous original New York Celtics. This team was just coming into the limelight when the Globe Trotters were disbanding in 1922-23. *Left to right:* Lapchick, Leonard, Dehnert, Barry, Holman, Whitty, Beckman, Burke.

(Below) The Grand Comedy Four. *Left to right:* Harry Fox, Basloe, Mike Brother, Jack Pryor.

Haggerty, Jack Nugent, Jimmy Davey, Jack Nolls, George Bell, and Sid Berger played with Troy.

Troy always featured a fast-passing game. The team early recognized that a ball could travel faster than a player and built up a fast and clever offensive system of short and long passes. The dribble was all but eliminated and passes were used to such effect that the infant game of basketball was almost revolutionized. They picked up where Bratton and Cooper had left off. Every player on the Troy team took part in the passwork. The center and guards, as well as the forwards, did a lot of the scoring. Defense for them meant the tight, man-to-man variety.

Among other innovations credited to Troy are the bounce pass, the short pass, the modern so-called "legal block," the fast break advancing the ball into scoring territory before the defense gets set, and the long pass from defensive territory into the offensive part of the court. The defensive guard did the feeding in this maneuver.

Later Ed Wachter spent twenty-five years in college—coaching at R.P.I., Williams, Harvard, and Lafayette. Lew Wachter went to Dartmouth, bringing the first Eastern Inter-Collegiate Championship to that college. Bill Hardiman served Union College throughout twenty successful seasons. Chief Muller coached at Manhattan College for many years.

It was teams like Troy and Trenton that fashioned the first principles of James Naismith and Lambert Will into rules that soon were adopted more or less throughout the country.

CHAPTER SEVEN

WE BECOME "WORLD CHAMPIONS"

IT WASN'T until the season of 1909–10 that I again had a team. That season I got together another group under the old magic name of the 31st Separate Company of Herkimer. There was Howard Bradshaw, Jack Andre of Frankfort, Brad Hall and James Conway of Utica, and Jim Murnane of Herkimer. This team was the best ever to represent the 31st, and it was one of the best I ever managed. This was the team that in 1911 beat the "unbeatable" Buffalo Germans, recognized "World Champions." The Germans had won 110 games without a defeat until the night they met the 31st.

Basketball had come to Buffalo in 1895. Frederick Burkhardt, a member of Naismith's Springfield team, brought it. The first team was the Junior Five, composed of Alfred Heerdt and Bill Rhode, forwards; John Maier, center; Edward Miller and Jay Bayliss, guards; and Emil Martin, substitute. In their first year this team was undefeated. That season set the pattern for the years to come. The next year they won 9 and lost none. Henry Faust replaced Jay Bayliss. In 1897 they lost their first games—3 out of 18. Edmund Reiman replaced Emil Martin.

From year to year their unbeaten record continued.

From 1900 to 1901 they played 33 games and lost only one. Their six-year total since first taking the floor was: 87 won and 6 lost.

In 1901 and 1902 the great Pan-American Exposition was held in Buffalo. In June of 1901 the first national open basketball tournament was played as part of the Exposition's athletic program. Teams entered included the highly favored Entres-Nons from Paterson, N. J.; the YMCA's from Brooklyn, Cambridge, and Newark; St. Joseph from Patterson, N. Y.; Flushing, L. I.; and the Buffalo team. The Buffalo team entered for the novelty of the thing. It would be good experience playing against these nationally rated teams, they thought.

As it turned out, it was an experience for the other teams to play against Buffalo. The first day of the tournament, on a clay court, Buffalo defeated Brooklyn 10 to 6. Then they defeated the highly favored Entres-Nons 16–5. The next day they defeated the Cambridge team 10 to 5. Then Newark went down by 9–3 and Flushing by 10–4. It was a clean sweep. But the team couldn't finish the tournament. Three of their players—Heerdt, Maier, and Reiman—were still attending the Mastin Park High School in Buffalo. They had to complete final exams before the Exposition play could be finished.

The Buffalo team wasn't called the "Germans" until it started its great winning streak in 1907–8. That season the team won 11 and lost none. In the 1908–9 season they won 40 straight without losing one. And included among the defeated teams were the Pacific Coast Champions from Dallas, Oregon, who had won 96 consecutive games and had traveled 10,000 miles before meeting the Germans. Buffalo also defeated Notre Dame that year.

Defeated but twice after this remarkable season, they went on to win 22 straight in 1909–10. Thirty-four more games were added to this record in 1910–12, and 23 more before they met my Herkimer team at Mohawk. My Herkimer lads showed the Buffalo boys how basketball was played in the Mohawk Valley. Before 2800 people, they beat the Germans 26–21.

Following this first defeat, the Germans bounced back to win 34 more games, losing only to Tonawanda, N. Y., and then going on to total 152 games won and only two lost. Before meeting the Herkimer team, they had won 110 straight—an all-time record. They scored 6001 points, an average of more than 54 points per game. No team ever scored more than 27 points in any one game against them.

They continued on as a team, occasionally adding young players and maintaining their prowess until they disbanded in 1929. A few of the stars who played later were Burt Post, Al Heerdt, Bill McCleary, Dip Murray, Ray Knapp, and Chuck Taylor. They won 761 games and lost 85 over a period of 29 years.

In 1931, when the average age of the men who had played on this team was 51, a benefit game was arranged at Tonawanda. Rhode, Heerdt, Schell, Miller, and Faust once again put on their uniforms and took to the floor. They beat the Tonawanda team by one point. Their physical condition was still so superb that three of them played the entire game of forty minutes, while the other two played one half each. They had only three nights of practice before the game. Two of these men were doctors, three were salesmen.

In June of 1912 Richard Dempsey of Oswego wrote asking me if I would like to come to Oswego and form a professional basketball team. The prospects seemed good and I accepted. Arrangements were completed by summer. Thus the Oswego Indians, later to become the famous Basloe Globe Trotters, came into being.

The remarkable center Oscar "Swede" Grimstead from New York City was on this team. He was tall, lanky, and fast. He had played amateur ball in New York City for several years, later joining the Paterson, N. J., professional team. He had also played with White Plains and Hudson in the Hudson River League and with Troy and Cohoes in the State League. Grimstead was the greatest ball handler in basketball. His style was that later used by the famous Harlem Globe Trotters.

The Mohawk Valley contributed most of the other players on this Oswego team. Jim Murnane was one of the stalwarts. There were six boys and two girls in the Murnane family, and four of the boys were basketball players— Ed, Jim, George, and Charlie. They were to Herkimer basketball what the Wachter family was to Troy. In the Wachter family it was Ed who was the great star. In the Murnane family it was Jim. Edward, Jim's twin brother, was a good player but he couldn't keep in condition like Jim. He quit the game and died at an early age. George also gave up the game while young to become a physician, later practicing in Utica. Charlie was an excellent college basketball, football, and baseball player. He became coach at Utica Free Academy and died at the height of a brilliant career. The city of Utica named one of its athletic fields in his honor.

Any one of these four brothers had ability enough to become a major leaguer in either baseball or basketball. Their father died while they were young. Only two of the boys, George and Charlie, got to college.

It was Jim who made the Murnanes famous in sports, especially in basketball. He started in 1900 as a lad of fourteen. In 1903 he played his first professional game with me on our trip to the great North Woods. Of the twenty years that Jim played the game, twelve of them were spent acting as captain of my teams. Each year he would help me select players for the coming season.

He was one of the all-time basketball greats. His defensive work (although he was a forward) was just as effective as his offensive work. Great forwards of the time hated to go against Jim Murnane. He invented the man-for-man style of play. Before each game he would get into a huddle with the players, explain the weaknesses and strong points of the opponents. "The sure way of winning," he would say, "is for each man to outscore his opponent."

The team never forgot his advice. Whenever our gang let down, he would yell for the whole crowd to hear, "You big boob, get out of the rocking chair!" or "What's the matter, you standing on a dime?"

Jim sent a large part of his earnings to his widowed mother. Always fair and honest, he was a great example to all the players who played with or against him. He was built so that if anyone got out of hand (as they sometimes did in games then) he could "cut them down to size." At the time he weighed 160 and stood five feet, seven.

Mike Roberts, another player I signed for Oswego, was one of the greatest running guards ever to play basketball. His real name was Mark Rabice and he came from a very poor Italian family in Utica. The only game in which he ever got really interested was basketball. From the first game he played he was popular with the crowds and a star on the floor. He started playing with School 19 (Washington School), Utica, in December, 1902. From there he went to the Schenectady Turners' team and St. Michael's semi-pro outfit.

His first stab at professional playing was with the Schenectady Continentals in 1907–8. The next season Mike came back to his home town to play with the 18th Separate Co. of Utica. At the time I made him an offer to play with

Oswego, Mike was boss machinist at the Utica Machine Company. Mike stayed with my teams for ten years without missing a season. It wasn't until 1922 that he left to become coach of the Muscatine, Iowa, team.

Mike enjoyed being the barber for our team. He would cut his toe nails with a straight razor and then shave his teammates with it—for nothing, if they could take it. He was very particular about the clothes he bought. Mike liked celluloid collars and little black shoestring bow ties. He always looked as though he had just been released from Ellis Island.

Roberts was a never-failing crowd pleaser. He was one of the best foul shooters in the business, too. In those days one man on the team did all the foul shooting. His record was thirty-three fouls in five games without a miss. Every dollar he could save went back to his parents, a lovely mother, an invalid father, a sick brother, and a sister. Mike's chief pleasure was smoking an Italian cigar or two each day, training or no training.

Mike made it a practice while on the road with the Globe Trotters always to buy the local paper of the town in which we were playing. This he would send back home for his folks to read. Had it not been for this habit of Mike's, many of the incidents in this book would have forever been forgotten.

In the summer of 1912 I bought an old open Hudson racing car for $300. I decided to have the car overhauled while I was in the West with the team; so I left the car at Mike's machine shop. Mike assured me they would do a good job "reasonable."

Next spring when I returned and went to the shop to pick up my car, they handed me a bill for $1200. Mike must have been sending them my financial statement each month so that they could charge accordingly. I argued them down to $800. Mike kept whispering in my ear, "Don't lose your dignity." I didn't. I lost $800.

Mike's specialty on the floor was "sucker shots" under the basket. When the play started from center, the ball would be tipped to the right forward, then back to Mike who, as a guard, wasn't expected to dash down the floor for a goal. But he did. This disconcerted the opposition. He perfected this play. In the days of the center jump after each goal, many high school and college coaches used the same play. Mike always shot on the run under the basket. This was a very pretty play to watch. With the elimination of the center jump in 1937, the play vanished.

At the forward position opposite Jim Murnane was Blubs Alberding. He was a real Mohawk Dutchman, short and chunky. He didn't look like a basketball player should look. But he was dangerous no matter where he played on the court. There were few better set shots. He had been with Utica, Fort Plain, and other State League teams before accepting my offer to play with the Indians. He stayed with me for three seasons.

Blubs Alberding had one guiding principle in his life: once you get a dollar, don't let it go. After he had saved a small amount playing basketball, his wife wanted a mink coat to show the relatives and girl friends how prosperous Blubs was. Blubs bought her the coat. It was well for his family's felicity that his wife couldn't tell the difference between skunk and mink. Blubs died when still a young man.

Johnny Murphy was standing guard on the Oswego team. His defensive work was unequalled at the time except maybe for that of Andy Suils of Troy.

The standing guard hardly ever scored a point. It wasn't his job to score. But it was his job to see that the other team didn't score. In those days, basketball was as much a defensive game as it was an offensive one. That's one reason scores were so low then compared with scores today. Johnny seldom went down the court to take a shot unless the defense was brought in so tight that he could slip right up to their basket safely.

The standing guard never left his position unless he was sure the running guard was there to replace him. All the plays in those days were started by the standing guard, but it was not unusual for a standing guard to play three or four games without taking a single shot.

The Oswego team first played together on November 12, 1912. Eighteen hundred people crowded the Oswego Armory to watch. Thereafter the Armory was packed on basketball nights. All through the winter famous New York State teams tried to beat the Indians. Few could.

Sometimes we played three games in a week. There were no movies. There was little theater. There were no dances except those following the games. Everyone who could, came to our games. It was *the* thing to do in Oswego that winter of 1912–13. In spite of the fact that the snow was piled so high one could not see across the street, they jammed the Armory. An hourly street car service was the only means of transportation.

All the games were played within the New York State League. At that time the teams in this league were the equal of any in today's National Association. If anything, the basketball played in 1912 was faster than that played today.

Towns and cities with teams included Gloversville, Troy, Cohoes, Glens Falls, Utica, Catskill, and Kingston. We beat all of them except Troy. The League had such stars as Barney Sedran, Marty Friedman, Lew Sugarman, Ed Wachter, Jack Inglis, Chief Muller, Jack Fox, Bill Hardman, Jimmy Williamson, John Cunningham, Johnny

Beckman, Pete Barry, Frank Bruggy, Flo Haggerty, Andy Soules, Toby Matthews, Lawrence Skiddy, Benny Bergman, Dick Leary, Jim Davey, Trim McInstry, Joe Fogarty, Jack Nolls, Cris Leonard, Skeets Wright, Jim Doyle, Stretch Meehan, Willy Cohen, Nat Holman, Ray Kennedy, Eddie Hallenbeck, Dewey Steffen, Hod Nestor, Bradley Hall, Al Schuler, Harry Riconda, Honey Russell, Bucky Harris, Pete Barry, Marty Barry, George Norman, Jakie Fuller, Carl and Dick Husta, Charles and Bill Powers, Jim Tome, and many others.

Barney Sedran of the Utica team was known as the "little runt of basketball." At the time, Barney was probably the smallest professional basketball player in the country, and he certainly must be included in any list of the all-time greats. He was small in size but "big at the gate." One night he was to play in Oswego against us. All the Utica players were in the dressing room but Barney. The manager, Jim Coughlin, was worried. He knew Barney had come along with the team. But game time was approaching and there was no sign of his star. Poor Barney had lagged behind the rest of the team on its way to the Armory. When he reached the entrance, Sergeant McDonald, who was taking tickets at the gate, refused to let him in. McDonald accused him of being a kid carrying a player's bag, and in Oswego (unlike the early days in Herkimer) this wasn't allowed. Barney insisted he wasn't a kid and that he was a player carrying his own bag. The Sergeant was unconvinced.

Manager Coughlin finally set out to find Barney. They met at the entrance. Barney was almost lost in a crowd of kids eager to see the evening's game, but lacking the funds. Even then, the Sergeant wouldn't let him in until I came out to vouch for him.

Barney was fun to watch, especially in the net. He was

fast and tricky and always a menace to Oswego's prowess on the court. As late as 1948 he was still coaching basketball.

Another team that came to Oswego to play us was the Metropolitan Five of New York City. It was made up of John Beckman, Frank Bruggy, Cris Leonard, Ernie Reich, and Mat Murray. In those days I had my stationery printed with "Oswego Indians" at the top. Swede Grimstead, a pal of these New York lads, wrote them about the "Indians." Bruggy wrote back to ask if Swede was playing with "real" Indians. Swede got a big laugh out of the letter and showed it around Tom Hennesey's Drug Store. "Shorty," the barber, Baker Sero, and John Kelly (lately retired Busy Corner of Utica traffic cop) were there at the time. They were ardent Oswego fans and they saw a chance to have some fun with the city slickers. So they formed a "tribe," along with Johnny White, the druggist at Hennesey's, and Swede.

Two games were arranged at Oswego with the Metropolitan lads. The team arrived from New York after traveling twelve hours. Cris Leonard had missed the train and Mike Donnelly, a Syracuse University player, took his place. He got to Oswego early and was let in on the plan.

Grimstead met the boys at the D. L. & W. Station. Nobody but the caretakers at the Armory suspected what we were up to. It was one of those real cold Upstate winter days—about 30 below and a great deal of snow. The city boys hurried to the Pontiac Hotel and didn't bother to investigate the Armory on a day like that.

Over at the Armory, Shorty and Jacky White were setting the scene, painting the faces of the Oswego team to look like Indians, mine included.

At the hotel, the New Yorkers wanted to know if we had a chief, and they were told yes, Chief Flat Foot Basloe.

Did they have squaws? Yes. Did they have schools? Yes, and a reservation about a mile out. Could they see the reservation? Yes, they could.

Shorty was contacted and he went down to his stable and pulled out a couple of old nags and hitched them to a sleigh. The Metropolitans piled into the sleigh and started out for what was really Fort Ontario. There was a light snow falling and it was fairly windy. When they finally arrived at the barracks they saw the gray stone walls, the low brown fort, and the smoke from the officers' mess hall. It looked authentic enough. The snow was coming down faster and faster. Shorty didn't take them any closer to the fort. Although the New Yorkers were disappointed at not seeing any Indians, they were satisfied that the Fort was a real reservation.

It was getting late. Shorty had accomplished his purpose of keeping the New Yorkers away from the Armory while the place was being fixed up. It was about 8:15 when they got back. As they walked across the drill shed floor toward their dressing rooms, they saw in the far corner a small pup tent. They didn't know it then, but Chief Flat Foot Basloe and his tribe were in that "tepee."

"Where in hell are the Indians?" demanded the Metropolitans. Shorty assured them that they stayed at the reservation at night and that the squaws were not allowed to come to town except on Saturdays. In the dressing rooms the New Yorkers proceeded to unpack revolvers which they stuck in the tops of their basketball pants before going onto the floor. They had come to shoot Indians!

Grimstead dressed with the New Yorkers. He explained that he never dressed with Indians. We waited until the Metropolitans came out onto the floor and began to practice. Then with a whoop and a holler we rushed out from our tepee and pranced around the floor like Indians. The spectators started screaming and yelling with delight. Shorty, the barber, the Oswego cheer leader, started Indian yells in the audience.

When the boys from Down-state saw this, they began to prance around, too, pulling the guns from their belts and firing them toward the ceiling. The Armory looked and sounded more like a Wild West show than a basketball game. The crowd never forgot that night. And just to prove Indians could play basketball, we whipped the Metropolitans in two games.

Bruggy was to become a catcher for the Philadelphia Athletics, and Reich, Leonard, and Beckman later became members of the world famous New York Celtics basketball team.

We arranged a championship series with the famous Buffalo Germans. Two games were to be played in Oswego on New Year's Day, 1912. My present that year was two victories on the same day over the Germans. Big holiday crowds of Oswegoians turned out to pack the Company D Armory. The team went after the Germans with everything they had. Every man was keyed up to his best. The teamwork was beautiful. Grimstead at center played the games of his life.

The afternoon crowd was not large, but it was in good voice. This first game was the more exciting of the two played. The teams battled on even terms most of the way. First one and then the other would score and the half closed with the score tied 12–12.

The first half was played under professional rules, while the second half was guided by association rules. But it was all the same to my Indians. They seemed to improve in the second half.

Miller of the Germans had his leg twisted and also got a wallop in the mouth from an Oswego player. But he deserved what he got. It was the kind of game in which "everything went." Oswego won 24–15.

New Year's night the two teams went at it again. The night game drew a crowd that taxed the Armory's capacity, equalling the largest crowd ever gathered in the building. It was a cheerful, cheering throng, and it had many opportunities to holler.

The Indians played in even better style than in the afternoon. They started off with a rush and soon had a commanding lead. The Germans made two baskets and a foul, but then we stopped them. At the end of the half the score was 12–5 in Oswego's favor. The second half under A.A.U. rules was somewhat slower. The Germans threw the ball all over the Armory, but it landed in the basket only occasionally. Oswego, however, had to be content with holding its early lead.

While Grimstead was the center of interest and outplayed the opposing center with ease, every man on the Oswego team played for all that was in him. Johnny Murphy hung on with bull-dog tenacity and spoiled many a German shot. Mike Roberts showed a brilliant brand of strategy and scored many great shots. Jim Murnane was in the game every minute, taking the ball from one end of the floor to the other. Blubs Alberding made some "impossible" shots.

The final score was 24–13—a nice Christmas present for any manager. Oswego was very happy with its Indians. The girls of Oswego were happy, too. The team featured for this game new plaid sweater coats which made a hit.

The season had been a big success. Newspapers all over the East acclaimed us one of the top teams in the country. At the close of that first successful season, the citizens of Oswego arranged a huge celebration in the Armory, scene of so many Oswego victories. Chamber of Commerce-like, the city realized that all the good publicity that came to it from the famous basketball team didn't hurt business a bit.

Joy in Oswego was short-lived, however. Oscar "Swede" Grimstead left the team. "Swede" had become something of a hero to the townspeople. The day before our last game that season (it was with Troy, which featured a new sensation in Jack Nolls, soon to replace Ed Wachter) "Swede" dropped into a local bar before the game and had quite a few beers. He went off to a livery stable, hired a horse and cutter, drove up to the door of the police station, and hitched Dobbin to the knob. Poor Swede. The local chief wasn't amused. In less than fifteen minutes Oswego's star center was in jail for the night.

On the floor the next evening there was something lacking in Swede's play, and as a result the whole team played indifferent, spiritless ball. They showed only flashes of the form they really possessed. Grimstead took little interest in the game. A far weaker team than Troy could have beaten us. Swede did not guard his man, Nolls, and he scored eleven goals for Troy. Troy won 41–33.

When Swede left, the town lost a hero. His departure created a hole in the lineup that was hard to fill. Not only was he a great ball player, he was also a great showman. The people loved him. A couple of years later he was playing for Utica in the State League.

To replace Swede I secured Raymond Bradshaw from Schenectady. He turned out to be a great center, also. Minn, as we called him, had a twin brother who also was a fine basketballer. But Howard was killed in an auto crash. Minn was best on defense, moving back after play started to cover our goal with Johnny Murphy. He was very good at picking off a man as he was dribbling down with the ball. Minn didn't lose many taps from center in his time. His father was a caretaker of a cemetery in

Schenectady. Minn himself was studying to be an embalmer at the time I signed him to the Indians.

Oswego in 1914 was not the Oswego of 1913. Even with a heavy downfall of snow and cold weather, January 1914 was much milder than January of the year before. The folks in town were also a lot milder in their support for the team. They didn't pack the drill shed as they had the year before to see the Indians play. This was due in large part to the absence of Swede Grimstead from the lineup. But the quality of ball we played was fully as good as that of 1913. Bobby Hammond, a former Colgate star, replaced Blubs Alberding.

By the time I had arranged for championship games with Buffalo, I was in the hole $700. The players were way back in their salaries. I was to get $200 for the two games that we scheduled against Buffalo. The boys were confident I would pay them just as soon as I got the money. So the team, at least, continued loyal.

On New Year's day of 1914 we played the Germans two games in Oswego before 4200 people with over a thousand turned away. It had been a long time since a sporting event stirred up the people of Oswego and Buffalo as this series did. It put new life into the flagging season. We won the first two games, 26–16 and 21–9. The third and fourth games were set for Buffalo on January 24 and 25.

The loyal fans of Oswego insisted on a big celebration the night before we left for Buffalo. Being superstitious, I vetoed the idea. It was like putting the cart before the horse. We should win first, then celebrate. The Germans would be no pushover.

A special train took at least 400 Oswego rooters to Buffalo for the contest the next day. As the Indians entered the Elmwood Music Hall where the game was to be played, the city fans started yelling: "Get the straw outa your pockets, you hayseeds!" About 4500 people were there each night. The band started playing "Why Girls Leave Home" as we came on the floor.

The folks from Oswego had no "Shorty the barber" to lead their cheers in return, but they made almost as much noise as the Buffalos. They weren't disappointed, either, for their Indians won the "World Championship."

We lost the third game at Buffalo 26–28. Murnane went out of the game with two sprained ribs. I had to go in as a replacement. But I didn't do too badly. I scored four points!

Murnane was strapped by Dr. Mansfield of Oswego and returned to play the next night. He was the hero of the game, playing under such a handicap. His appearance inspired the team to victory. We won 26–22. It was the first time the Germans had ever been defeated on their home court.

The $200 guarantee I received at Buffalo didn't stay long in my hands, however. The constable of Hamilton, N. Y., was in the audience and followed me to the dressing room afterwards. He held out his hand and demanded $200 for back room rent and board at Colgate University. It seems that our star forward Bobby Hammond thought his manager should pay his back bills. Bobby used to wait on tables and wash dishes in school, but some way or other he neglected to pay $200 worth of debts. I said to the constable, "Listen here, it's awful easy for me to get impatient."

"As long as I get my $200 I don't care what you get," the constable replied.

So now I was in the hole $900. The players all liked Bobby and said he was a good player and a regular fellow. I asked him if he didn't know he was in debt at Colgate.

"You can't expect me to know everything," he replied.

Bobby had been a sensation for the Red Raiders. He could hit the basket from almost any point on the floor and could dribble past the best defense. He was greatly responsible for many of the victories on our forthcoming trip. The $200 was well spent, as it turned out, because Bobby was to prove invaluable in many of our future games.

That summer he signed to play with the Cleveland Indians as a second baseman and thereafter played baseball instead of basketball. Bobby died early in a brilliant career.

By winning the "World's Basketball Championship" the Oswego team became famous throughout the country. Offers came in from points in the East, South, and West to play local teams. Every team manager wanted the Oswegos to make an appearance. They drew crowds wherever they went.

I was undecided about accepting any offers. Here was guaranteed fortune. Here was guaranteed prestige. But traveling on the road throughout the Midwest would be a new experience for me and for the boys on my squad. I was only twenty-six years old, and the boys were even younger.

On the other hand, if I refused the chance now that I had a winning team, I might never again have the opportunity. It was take it now or never. I took it. The boys agreed. We prepared to blaze new trails out West. I arranged a schedule, took the best offers, bought the tickets, and began one of the most exciting and rewarding adventures of my life.

CHAPTER EIGHT

GO WEST, YOUNG MEN

So we were "World Champions." We had defeated the Buffalo Germans. But nobody had handed us a silver loving cup. We were "Champions" in name only. It was a mythical title. No certificates, no "series money," no nothing.

I felt we should have some evidence we really were "World Champions." I was walking along a busy street in Buffalo thinking about this problem when I happened to pass an F. W. Woolworth Five-and-Ten Store. There, prominently displayed in the window, was a collection of felt banners emblazoned with "Philadelphia Athletics, World Championship." In those days the A's had championship teams. In October, 1913, they had conquered the New York Giants in the World Series to gain the "World Championship."

I had an idea. If I could just remove "Philadelphia Athletics" from these pieces of three-cornered felt, I would have my "World Championship," ready made. Sure enough, the "A's" weren't stuck too tight on the banners. They came off with little effort. So I bought twelve.

The players were delighted. Each received a banner for his part in winning the German game. The rest of the banners I kept in my suitcase, neatly rolled up in a corner. They came into good—if unusual—use later on in our westward trek.

Once decided, we didn't waste time heading West. This was in spite of the fact that every man on the team was crippled after that German game. Roberts had a bad leg, Murnane's ribs were in bad shape, Murphy's leg was swollen and he was in no condition to play. Hammond suffered from a wrenched hip and Bradshaw had a charley horse. The team bandaged up each other before each game.

The day after downing the Germans, we started. None of us had ever been farther west than Buffalo. None of us knew what lay ahead. We were, to tell the truth, a bunch of backcountry yokels going into the big cities for the first time. We were ignorant about the ways of the world, but we had country boys' curiosity about everything we saw and did. We got "taken in" many times. Sharpers took advantage of our ignorance. But we had a wonderful time just the same—maybe because we were so innocent. A little country pluck got us out of a good many scrapes.

It was about this time that I undertook to write letters back home to the *Utica Press* and Paul Williams, its editor, on the progress of the team. At every stop I would write Paul. He would print the letters in his paper so everyone in central New York rich enough to buy the *Press* could follow the "World Champions" as they battled the best in the Midwest.

As we rode west that day, I grew very nervous thinking about the future. The novelty of this trip, the inexperience of both players and myself, didn't improve my stomach. I had six tickets worth $80, one for each player and myself, clutched in my hand. I stared out the window lost in thought. The telephone poles flashed by monotonously.

I forgot what I was doing and began chewing up the tickets!

Suddenly the conductor was there asking for fares. I looked in dismay at the tattered fragments of cardboard in my hand. As the conductor asked each player for his ticket, the player would point to me and say, "There's the manager." I closed my fist tightly around the remains. The conductor came to me.

"Tickets?"

I opened my hand and showed him the fragments.

"What happened, were you hungry?" he asked in surprise.

"No."

"Did you hold up the ticket office in Buffalo?"

"Of course not."

"How can anyone in his right mind eat that many railroad tickets? You sure you didn't swallow a couple?"

"No, sir."

"Who do you represent?"

"The world champion Oswego basketball team."

"Have you anything to show for it?"

I pointed to my team.

"I mean any credentials or certificates or diplomas," the conductor persisted.

"Just a moment," I said. I opened my bag and dug around until I found a world championship banner. I showed it to the conductor. He looked at it for a moment, felt it, then turned to me.

"That's all right for you. What about the others?"

So the other six dug into their bags and produced their own world championship banners which I had given them in Buffalo. The trainman seemed satisfied. He took what was left of my tickets and put them into a little envelope as if they were precious, decayed pieces of parchment.

Then he put his hand into his pocket and brought something out. "Here's something you can have so this won't happen again."

"What is it?" I asked.

"A plug of Black Jack chewing tobacco."

"Thanks, I don't chew. I just smoke."

"Try it, my boy, it will come in handy."

I took it. "What can I do for you, conductor?" I asked.

"How about one of those world championship banners for a souvenir?"

"Yes, sir. The best-looking one I have. But, conductor, please don't sell it to the railroad company."

Just outside Cleveland our train was sidetracked for quite a while. We sat for a long time waiting for the trouble up ahead to be cleared up. We were unable to get out and see the city for fear of missing the train. Trouble came to us.

The next stop was to have been Ada, Ohio. But I discovered that I didn't have enough money to get there. The team had to get on to Lima that night. I took the conductor aside. He asked for our tickets. I said that was what I wanted to talk about to him. I didn't dare tell him the only tickets I had were from a Chinese laundry in Buffalo.

He asked me to wait until he had gone through the rest of the coaches. The team didn't know what a scrape we were in. They were enjoying the Ohio scenery (Cleveland railroad yards) outside the windows. It was like an excursion—to them. That is, until a bullet suddenly crashed through a window and ricocheted over the head of Mike Roberts. It just wasn't Mike's day to die. A railroad detective was chasing a bum in the yards. The bum had a gun. The cop and the bum began firing. The conductor, who had just returned from punching tickets, decided we could delay our talk for a while. We all took up positions on the floor. If that shot had been a little lower, we would have had to look for another barber.

When the gun play moved off down the tracks, we again took our seats. The conductor turned out to be a philanthropist. I told him our story. We had just won the "World Championship" in basketball. We had been forced to give up $200 of our Buffalo fee because one of our players had neglected to pay his board bill. We had to be in Lima that night.

At first, he thought we were giving him the old runaround and that we were just a bunch of broken-down actors. He's had experience with that sort before.

To prove our point, I had the boys haul out their uniforms. These convinced him. He agreed to consider us twelve-year-olds and let us ride for half price. He even saw to it that we had a few dollars left just in case anything happened in Ada. He was a real friend. I was just getting acquainted with the world and its troubles. We had come close to being put off the train. Only the kindness of the conductor had saved the "World Champions" from an ignominious fate.

We couldn't eat in the dining car with the well-to-do people. We had to be content with ham and cheese sandwiches, milk or coffee. This had to be our fare until we got back on our feet and could latch onto some real guarantees. It was up to the team to produce and they knew it. Either they won or we didn't eat well. I'd thought that when we became "World Champions" we would be able to go into a diner and do a lot of other things champions did. What pipe dreams! Right at that moment, we were in the same predicament as any group of broken-down vaudeville performers on the one-night-stand beat.

Just as we were leaving Cleveland, Bobby Hammond exclaimed, "Well, boys, this is where I am going to hang out next summer. I wish you would all drop in to see me."

Bobby had been signed to play with the Cleveland Indians. I had suggested that Bobby get off the train in Cleveland and contact the Indians' manager. Maybe he could have helped us. No soap. We had to struggle on the best we could. Anyway, if Hammond continued to be the star he was in Buffalo, our future meal checks were assured.

I don't think the little town of Ada was named for a civilized woman. Ada must have been quite a dame. What a hotel! It was probably built by an Indian about the time Columbus bumped into America. The rooms were pips. Doors swung on one-screw hinges. It had dirty water. It had kerosene lights that smoked up the dingy little rooms in the night in less time than it took to find the chamber pot under the bed.

The bathroom was out of this world—almost. It was at least a hundred yards from the hotel! That night before we went to bed we drew straws to see who would be first in the morning to "pay his respects." This was the first time in my life I ever won drawing straws.

I made arrangements with the owner of the hotel (he was also janitor and bartender) to borrow his heavy fur overcoat, fur hat, and overshoes the next morning after he brought in the wood for the two big oak stoves and got the fires started.

I got up at 6 A.M. I looked out the window. Snow had fallen all night. The drifts were very high in spots. It was terribly cold. I saw the proprietor outside with fur coat, fur hat, and overshoes just starting his hundred-yard march to the wood pile and outhouse. I wanted to make the hundred-yard march, too, but had to wait until the fur coat, the fur hat, and the overshoes returned.

At the wood pile the man got an armful of kindling and started back. Then he stopped, dropped the wood, and returned to the outhouse. At the door he stopped, turned around, and set off for the wood pile.

"Make up your mind," I said to myself. The room was ice-cold. It was no time to stand around. Nor was I going to open the window and yell. The icy blast would have frozen me.

The man picked up the wood again and started back to the hotel. "Thank God," I muttered. He got halfway, suddenly dropped his load, turned, and raced for the outhouse. I went back to bed in disgust.

At breakfast that morning I ruined the budget with a breach of Midwestern etiquette. The waitress brought in a large bowl of Grapenuts and set it down in front of me with a pitcher of cream. I poured most of the cream on the cereal and began eating. The rest of the team sat around the table looking hungry.

"What's the matter, boys," I asked. "Aren't you going to have any cereal?"

The waitress came back. "Don't you know that bowl is for all the boys?" she demanded rather tartly.

It cost me a nickel extra to get five more dishes of Grapenuts. A nickel out of our budget at that time was a big hole. The hotel charged 25¢ for breakfast, 50¢ for dinner, and 75¢ for the double-beds. Incidentally, we beat Ada 28–20.

Our next stop was Lima, Ohio. We beat the White Stars on their home court, the first time that had happened that season. During the first half of that game the play was fierce and very rough. The partisan crowd soon began to hoot and jeer us. A couple of fights started but were quickly broken up by the officials.

Our unique defense stopped the Lima forwards completely. Whenever the Stars would recover the ball in our territory and before they could get away with it into the vicinity of their goal, Murnane, our captain, would have some of our men instantly in line with him across the center of the floor. The barricade thus formed divided the local team. The forwards under the basket would be closely watched by guards and the remainder of the Stars would be cut off from their territory by the barricade. Time and again they tried rushing our line, but they seldom succeeded.

Bobby Hammond's goal shooting that night was sensational. Whether a long shot or rushing the ball up under the basket, he missed very few times. The Lima boys played well and hard. But they couldn't solve our defense. The final score was 36–18 in our favor.

As the Lima sports writer put it:

Every man of the Oswego Indians is a finished athlete. Big, well-built, muscular, well-proportioned and full of speed and strength, the New Yorkers possess all the qualities of a championship team. Every man . . . is a mountain of strength. Bradshaw at center is a regular fortress in himself, and the remaining four of the squad are right on his heels when it comes to possessing the ability of genuine basketball players. Hammond and Murnane are dead shots . . . from any position on the floor, while Murphy and Roberts are regular war-horses in the guard work. The entire company knows the full meaning of that word "teamwork," which is a most essential factor in winning any game.

This writer couldn't get over the fact we stood up so well to the rough-and-tough tactics of the local team. He went on:

Another asset of no less value to the Oswego boys is their nerve. Judging from the amount of nerve displayed by the Oswego athletes last night, Uncle Sam would do well to send them down to Mexico to clean up the mess. Playing a game of "give and take" the visitors could not be made to quit for a moment. Hammered and battered in the many hard games indulged in during their trip through this part of the country, the Oswego players are bruised and scratched up to the extent that bandages compose a big portion of their uniforms. But they seem to have been raised on rough stuff. The rougher the game grew the more they seemed to like it. If one of the Stars got peeved over the roughness and planted his fist somewhere on a visitor's map, the Oswego would merely return the compliment and play that much harder.

Undaunted by the wild rooting of the hundreds who packed the auditorium, and only spurred on by the hot remarks of the spectators, the visitors, cool-headed and calm, tore in right away and steadily broke down both the offense and defense of the locals.

And as to the Stars—well, it is no disgrace for them to go down before the great Oswego aggregation.

We stayed in Lima until Sunday morning. Saturday evening we were guests of Miss Mabel Faulkner and a number of her girl friends. An informal program was given during the party. Bobby Hammond played the piano; Murnane told stories of his life and funny experiences he had had. Bradshaw recited poetry and Mike Roberts gave a little sketch of the old barber shop back home. Then Johnny Murphy and I put on a vaudeville hit, "School Days," which used to be part of my act when I was on the stage. Lima wasn't all basketball.

While at Lima I received a telegram from Fond du Lac, Wisconsin, offering me $300 to play three games there. The team was eager to make the trip. But I held out for more. I wired back asking for $400. By 6 o'clock of the Saturday night of the game with the White Stars, I had not received any reply. I was disappointed. We were to play Fort Wayne Sunday afternoon and Chicago Sunday night. If we didn't get that telegram, we would have to return East after Chicago.

Finally I decided to take the $300. It would save the trip.

Playing Fond du Lac, one of the greatest teams in the West, would add to our prestige and would probably lead to more games. I really couldn't afford to refuse the offer. But I thought we were being underpaid.

At Fort Wayne I was forced to play a whole game. Poor Murnane got so bruised up in the Lima battle that he would not play. I told him he had to play. He insisted he wouldn't play. We argued for about ten minutes. Then he, as team captain, overruled the manager. I had to put on a uniform.

I wasn't the player that Jim Murnane was. Some strategem had to be worked out so the Fort Wayne team would not take us for an easy victory. After all, we were "World Champions" and had to keep up a good front. It wouldn't do to take too many defeats from locals.

This called for public relations work. I was to be star of the team. When the Fort Wayne reporters came into the dressing room for advance news, they were all directed to me. I was pointed out as an All-American.

As I was putting on my uniform, two men approached me and introduced themselves as reporters from the local paper. Mike Roberts and Jim Murnane began talking. They said I was one of the greatest players in the country. A terror on the floor. A superb shot. With speed of lightning. Tremendous endurance. Aggressive. Tough. Unbeatable.

It had its effect. The two approached me with awe. They began asking questions, respectfully, like men talk to the President of the United States or their congressmen. They wanted to know how I became a great star, how long I had played basketball, whom I had outpointed, and how many points had been scored on me. Jim and Mike went off and muffled giggles at the other end of the locker room.

But I was equal to the occasion. I acted as though talking about myself was a great bore and bother. No, I couldn't remember how many points I'd scored—there were just too many. I couldn't remember how many points had been scored on me—it was so long ago since it had happened. I had been in basketball "for quite a few years." About my being a star? Well, I modestly admitted that I was pretty good. "When I start shooting, no matter where I am on the court, I don't even touch the rim," I boasted.

They thought this quite remarkable.

"It don't make any difference how long the court is, either," I put in.

They couldn't understand how a man could shoot so well. I built them up to the idea that I was the greatest star in the country. The strategy worked. Word reached the opposing Fort Wayne squad of the star that was to play against them. They assigned their best player, a man by the name of Robinson, to guard me. He was supposed to do all in his power to make sure I didn't score.

Well, as it happened, I wasn't such a bad shot after all. I wasn't the player that Jim Murnane was, but that night, at least, I found the range.

The game began. Bradshaw tapped the ball to Mike Roberts. He shot it back to me. With nothing better to do with it, I aimed it for the basket. In it went—without touching the rim! Three times in ten minutes this happened. Robinson decided he'd have to watch me all evening and not do any shooting himself. As a result all their plays and signals were crossed up. By never letting me shoot again Robinson deprived his team of his offensive skill, and my team crashed through the Fort Wayne defense time and time again, scoring easily. By the time it was over, we had scored 32 points to Fort Wayne's 14. . . . The flat-footed manager proved he could be just as valuable on the floor as off.

That evening we played the Monarch Athletic Association of Chicago and won 14 to 12 in the last minute of play. Bobby Hammond came through with one of his sensational set shots from the middle of the court. At the end of the second half both teams had been tied at 12–12. It was decided to play until one team or the other made a basket—a "sudden death" type of rule. That's when Bobby came through.

After the game a great many fans told us how eager they were to see the Fond du Lac series. These games were becoming the topic of every sports conversation in the Midwest.

Fond du Lac had quite a history in basketball. Basketball was first played there in the fall of 1896 by members of Company E, Second Wisconsin National Guard unit. They used seven men on a team. In the season of 1898–99, after the Company returned from the Spanish American War, the game was taken up in a big way, with Roy Rogers as coach and forward and the great A. G. "Butch" Brunkhorst at the other forward.

By the next year the team was recognized as just about the best in the Midwest. That season Yale had probably the best team in the East. A series was arranged between these two basketball giants to be played in Fond du Lac during the college boys' Christmas vacation. It was to decide the "Championship of the United States."

Yale played two games enroute from Connecticut, one at Washington and one at Pittsburgh. On the way from Pittsburgh to Fond du Lac their train was held up back of a wreck. They got into Chicago too late to make a train to Fond du Lac. So the Wisconsin Central Railroad (now the Sioux Line) ran a special train up to Fond du Lac to get them there—only an hour late. Such was basketball interest then!

Reserved seats for these famous contests were sold out long before the dates of the games. General admission seats went on sale at 6 A.M. the day of the game. Fans brought their lunches with them and formed lines a block long. Many hundreds were turned away each night. The auditorium would seat only about 1400 people.

And though Yale brought a whole staff of coaches and trainers and even their own drinking water from New Haven, they lost all three games. It should be noted, however, that the team had had a hard trip.

Basketball in the Midwest got quite a boost from this Yale series. Fond du Lac got a national reputation, and other towns around began recruiting basketballers.

The Fond du Lac *Daily Reporter* headlined the Yale defeat thus: "Yale Players Return to Their Studies with New Ideas in Their Heads." The article continued: "Yale came here with the assurance of victory that crack college teams usually take with them wherever they go. There were some Fond du Lac people who also fully believed that Yale would win from the soldiers. But at no time did the wearers of the red suits allows the Easterners to come anywhere near taking a game."

The series was played according to Yale's interpretation of the basketball rules, and was, therefore, very rough. Wrist holds were allowed and Yale players were permitted to grapple with the soldiers almost as much as they wished. Very few fouls were called unless they were so flagrant that they could not help but be noticed. In other words, Yale was given every opportunity to do just such playing as they had been used to down East. Of course, the soldiers could use grappling and wrist holds too. They did.

Here are the scoring totals of the third game. Note how few fouls were called, even though it was considered one of the roughest games ever played in the area.

Fond du Lac				Yale			
	Free Throws	Field Goals	Called Fouls		Free Throws	Field Goals	Called Fouls
Rogers	5	2	0	Clark	0	4	4
Brunkhorst	0	2	0	Todd	0	0	1
Bruett	0	3	0	Sharpe	1	0	1
Brunet	0	1	2	Rodgers	0	1	1
Buch	0	0	1	Finc	0	1	1
	—	—	—	Hyatt	0	0	1
Totals	5	8	3		—	—	—
				Totals	1	6	9

Total points 21   Total points 13

Referee: R. L. Harriss of Milwaukee

Other fine teams were organized throughout the West. There was Company D of Ripon, Company G of Appleton, Battery A of Milwaukee, Stevens Point, and Port Washington—all of Wisconsin. There were the Red Men of Red Wing, Minnesota, and the talented Muscatine, Iowa, team. The Fond du Lac and Ripon teams were such rivals that many times special trains were run to take the teams and fans to the games.

The Fond du Lac teams, however, did not preserve the high caliber of the 1900 organization. Then in 1911–12 Charles Wright was made manager of the Company E team and George Fogarty, former New York National star, was made player-coach. Together they started to rebuild Fond du Lac to its former power and prestige. In the next three years Fond du Lac played 119 games, won 110, and lost only 9. In 1913–14 (the season we first played them) they won 39 straight games.

George Fogerty, with his dribble, short pass, and pivot, was their outstanding player—one of basketball's all-time greats.

The team played the 1914–15 season under the management of Jack Brunkhorst with great success. They lost only to my Globe Trotters and the famous Troy team under Lew Wachter.

After the 1914–15 season the Mexican border trouble came up and Company E went south for some time. It eventually went overseas in World War I and that was the end of Company E basketball.

Major Trier of Fond du Lac was the first American major killed in the war. He had been a member of the E team that defeated Yale. There were other good teams after the First War, but none had the record of the old Company E team. Green Bay, Racine, Princeton, Appleton, Winona, Ashland, New London, Manitowoc, Sheboygan, Jamesville, Washburn, Monroe, Portage, La Crosse, Tomah, Nenah Meenasha, Plymouth, Beloit, and Oshkosh were among the best.

On our journey from Chicago to Fond du Lac, we learned from the conversation of passengers on the train that many were on their way to see us play. We met a priest who had seen the championship games in Buffalo. His home was in Fond du Lac and he was sure his home town had the greatest team in the country.

When we arrived at the Fondy railroad station, we found that transportation to our hotel had been provided. There stood a beautiful gray mare hitched to the local cab. It was 20 below zero. We wasted no time heading for the cab. But all of us couldn't fit inside. It would only hold five. Guess who had to ride out in the breezes with the driver? . . . But I didn't mind too much.

As we drove by the Armory where the game was to be played, I saw hundreds of people standing in line, waiting to get tickets. Remember, it was 20 below zero!

I inquired of the cab driver about the town, the people, the team, and everything else I could think of. The driver was almost seven feet tall. I told him about our team, how we had won the championship from the Germans, how we had "mowed down" all opposition between here and

Buffalo, and what stars we all were. A little public relations never hurt, I thought.

We registered at the hotel, stored our luggage, had a light lunch, and headed for the Armory. We found ourselves in a Midwestern Madison Square Garden. Thirty-five hundred people were jammed into the drill shed. There wasn't an empty seat to be seen. To our surprise, we saw the first basketball cage since leaving New York State. There was a four-foot fence all around the playing floor and a large rope cage hanging from the balcony around it. There were glass backboards. The Westerners never heard of playing basketball with open baskets.

The cage, of course, allowed no out-of-bounds balls. It also made it impossible for the spectators to interfere with the players or referee—no small consideration in those days of "audience participation" basketball.

My team made the first appearance on the floor. A few minutes later Company E came out in very beautiful uniforms. Their center, Ben Hawkins, six feet, eight inches tall, turned out to be the cab driver who had so courteously let me talk on about our team on the way from the station.

Half the crowd, especially in the general admission seats in the balconies, must have come very early. They had lunches with them. Many had traveled over miles of windswept country roads to see this game. I was more certain than ever that I needed a bigger guarantee than $300 for three nights. I was also certain that if I didn't demand more *before* the game was over, I would never get more. I had only $12 left in my pocket after the trip from Chicago.

The game began. Murnane got the first basket after two minutes had gone by. Then he got another before the locals could score. Fogarty raced in to make the score 4–2.

Then the scoring went back and forth for the remainder of the first half. At this point we lead 16–7.

Something had to be done if I was to get more money. It would be a gamble to wait longer. I approached Manager Wright.

"You know, you're not paying me enough money for this game," I said.

"Now, Mr. Basloe," he replied, "I will take care of you after the game is over."

Well, I thought, if the first game wasn't a success, it might hurt attendance for the final two games. If it turned out well, Wright might give me another $50, but no more. I had to put the heat on.

Since my presence was no longer needed on the floor, I went up into the crowded balcony during the half-time intermission. Many of the people had left their seats. I wanted to irritate the fans there. They had enough leftovers from their lunches so that, if they used them to serenade the team, it would cause a riot. That's what I wanted.

To some of the fans who had been standing up since 6:30 eating their lunch I said, "Those New Yorkers think that we Fond du Lac people are a bunch of farmers. I wish I had an armful of garbage. I would let them have it for sure."

In no time I had an armful of half-eaten lunches. I had to leave as I saw the teams coming back onto the floor, but the crowd was sufficiently aroused by that time so that the least bit of rough stuff would set them off.

I went down to join my players. I got them into a huddle and told them, "Boys, rough it up a little bit. Let these people know they're seeing a real game."

The second half started. Fond du Lac began to hit a stride which took them to within three points of us. Then it happened. The score was 16 to 13. The ball was at the north end of the hall and nearly every player on the floor was after it. It was a scrimmage that would have done credit to football. Fogarty had wormed his way into the mass and was emerging with the ball when Roberts tackled him. Fogarty brushed him aside and Mike, off balance, took a spill.

The crowd in the balcony came through. A rain of garbage came down on the players. I jumped up, stopped the game, and called my team off the floor.

The crowd got more unruly than ever. I accused the referee of using Mexican rules. He got sore. Jim Murnane then turned on him and yelled, "Why don't you get a rocking chair?"

The fireworks were popping. I herded the team into the dressing rooms. The fans crowded after us, calling us every name in the Bible and some more that weren't in there. I told the manager, "We're going to take the first train home."

When we finished dressing and were ready to head for the hotel, the crowd became more menacing. It looked as though a real riot was brewing. The balcony rooters spotted me as the guy who had cheered for Fond du Lac. This didn't cool their anger.

Finally I insisted that Captain Trier of the Company E squad call out the militia to escort us to the hotel. He obeyed and a squad of twenty soldiers formed a hollow square around us.

As we entered the hotel lobby, Captain Trier, Manager Wright, and Jack Brunkhorst called me aside. I was afraid they were going to claim the championship by forfeit and tell us to go ahead and take the next train home, and I was wondering how $12 would get the six of us all the way to

New York. But Wright came through. He knew that ten thousand people were waiting to see these two teams play.

"Now, what's the holdup, Basloe? How much is it going to cost me for the next two games?"

I was all out of breath. I said, "Twelve hundred more." In other words, $1500 for the series.

I looked at Wright. I thought the poor manager might need propping any minute. But he took it like a major—or rather captain. He agreed to pay me the $1500. Then I had all *I* could do to stand up. A check for that amount was certified and put in the bank.

That night and during the next day, as news of the first night's outcome spread through the states of Wisconsin, Minnesota, and the Dakotas, offers for games flooded in to me. How different it would have been had I stayed and finished the game—and been defeated. This was the turning point in our financial affairs. At the end of the third game that Saturday the management and fans of Fond du Lac presented me with a cowboy suit and gun. I was christened The Holdup Manager. However, the first game was given to Fond du Lac by forfeit, 2–0.

There was an interesting little sidelight on this riot. One George Brown, a spectator at the Armory that night, got into a fight with a crowd of young fellows who occupied seats in the balcony. Brown was arrested after he freely admitted that he was the aggressor. But the next day in court, Brown's excuse was that he had been "roasted" for rooting for Fond du Lac and that he had started his fisticuffs only after being informed that he was "as yellow as Company E." These mitigating circumstances were fully taken into consideration by Fond du Lack Judge Blewett. He imposed a $1 fine, the minimum possible for the disorderly conduct charge. The trouble was the first of its kind that had occurred in the audience during a basketball game, the Fond du Lac management announced, and "it is much regretted. . . ."

We won the next game, 26–24, and Fond du Lac won the third, 28–20. For this Manager Wright wanted a World Championship Banner. I put him off with a promise that he should wait thirty-five years and then I would send it for Christmas. Thirty-five years later I received a card on Christmas Day demanding the banner. In fact, he came to Herkimer after it.

The next stops after this were Green Bay, Neenah-Menasha, and Appleton. We were very much impressed with the beauties of these towns, particularly since we won all three games.

Present day basketball players, with modern gymnasiums and transportation facilities at their disposal, may find it difficult to visualize the conditions under which men were forced to play the game in these early years.

The roomy, comfortably-heated motor coaches which travel fast and keep out the icy blasts were far in the future fifty years ago. Where steam trains or trolley connections made the use of such vehicles possible, travel in the old days was not so bad. But in many parts of the country —such as Wisconsin—pioneer basketball players had to depend on horses and sleighs.

Many people today, I suppose, can remember traveling to the big game in a sleigh. When roads were good and nights were clear, the rides were fun. Half a dozen or more big sleighs filled with boys and girls often made the trips. There were worse ways to spend the evening than returning home from the big game wrapped in a warm fur robe with your best girl, sleighbells jingling, and snow glistening under a full winter's moon.

But when roads were drifted full and the traveling athletes were forced to use snow shovels to get through to the next town, the trips were anything but pleasant. One basketball team traveling by sleigh in the late 1890's from one New England town to another got lost in a snowstorm and three members of the party died from exposure.

Games were played under conditions almost impossible for present-day players to believe. The only halls available in many of the smaller towns were lighted by flickering kerosene lamps and heated by big stoves usually located in one corner of the room. These courts were small with slippery floors. It was not uncommon for players to be shoved against a hot stove at the end of the court. Shower baths were undreamed of in most communities. Players were forced to dress and undress in unheated rooms. Men had to be men to stand the gaff.

Our next stop was Minneapolis, where we had agreed to play another series. We got our train at Milwaukee. After riding for a while, the dining car looked very inviting; so we all trouped into the car and sat down. It was the first time any of us had ever been in a dining car. The only miscue we made was drinking the water in the finger bowls. After the waiters had had a good laugh, they told us of our mistake.

Minneapolis was colder than Fond du Lac. Here it was 30 below. In our thin topcoats we literally suffered from the cold. We stayed in the West Hotel, a beautiful old-fashioned building of fine, large graystone blocks. We were to play ten games in seven days—two games with the Ascension Club, two with the St. Joseph Club, two with the City Club, two with the Company D team, one game at Chaska, Minn., and two games at Red Wing. That was a killing schedule for sure.

Of these ten games, we lost only two—one to the Ascensions (we also won one from them) and the other to the team of the little town of Chaska. They beat us 30–27, to our own and everyone else's amazement.

After finishing this series, we headed back for two more games with Fond du Lac. Company E wound up its regular season by beating us in the final game after we had won the first game 28–23.

That final game the next day was spectacular. Toward the close the excitement became intense. We pulled off a whirlwind finish. With but six minutes to play and with Fond du Lac leading 20–10, we began to score. Roberts, Hammond, and Murnane suddenly brought us to within two points of the lead. Then Fondy scored a foul. Then Murnane scored a goal. The score was 20–21. With two seconds to play, a double foul was called. If Mike, our foul shooter, made his throw and Fondy's shooter failed to make good, the game would undoubtedly go into overtime.

The crowd was whooping it up. The Armory was filled with sound. Mike walked up to the foul line and tossed up his shot. The ball struck on the rim, rolled crazily about for a few seconds—and then dropped out.

Then the Fondy player advanced with the ball. He made his throw. It was perfect. The ball dropped through without hitting the rim. Men, women, and children screamed and shouted. The ball was put in play, but in a matter of seconds the whistle blew. The game was finished. Fond du Lac easily had the best team in the West, possibly one of the best teams in the nation at the time.

There was one other contest on this return trip home that must be mentioned. I engaged the team to replay the Lima White Stars. The Stars were still sore about the defeat we had inflicted on them on our way out West. Lima got everything ready for revenge.

The game was rough throughout and developed into a

near riot during the second half when Bradshaw and the Lima center Bolin started swinging at each other. For a few seconds they pounded each other viciously. Then other players and spectators rushed in to separate them. One or two of the spectators started to take up the argument, but the referee and the players managed to break it up. The rest of the players kept their heads and refrained from further delaying the game with personal grievances.

Poor Jim Murnane had slipped early in the game and badly damaged his right eye. During the fight he had rushed in to help Brad and received another punch in the same eye. This put him out cold for the rest of the game. Since we carried no substitutes, we had a problem as to who would play. Luckily "Skeet" Hill of the Company G team of Ada was in the audience. He agreed to put on an Oswego uniform. He played a swell game, too, considering he had never practiced with us before and was unfamiliar with our style of play.

One of the unique features of the game was the alteration of rapid offensive playing and close and guarded defensive work. The Stars had developed a number of ways to break our defense. Time and again the defensive barricade which we set up across the middle of the floor was made useless through the schemes of the locals.

In fact, it was so much of a defensive game (unlike today's free scoring parades) that Bradshaw during the whole game never took a shot at the basket. He devoted his entire time to guarding the opposing center, Bolin.

From the beginning everyone realized the score would be low and the game a close one. The final score was 16–10 in favor of the White Stars. Without Murnane we did not have one of our chief scoring punches.

At one time during the game some fans asked me to take my team off the floor so they could have their money back. But the players insisted upon sticking as long as anyone could stand up. There was only one man left un-injured at the end. It was the worst treatment we had ever received on the road. A lot of money was bet on the game and that may have caused some of the trouble.

It was here at Lima that I first got the idea of selling my World Championship pennants. After the game the Lima manager came over and wanted me to hand over to him my World Championship pennant. He'd heard we had won one for defeating Buffalo.

"We're the champions now," he exclaimed. "We'd like the pennant."

"You mean you want the Championship for Lima?" I asked. I was dumfounded. But not for long. I had an idea. "How much is it worth to you?" I asked him.

"I don't know," he said. "How much do you want?"

"Fifty dollars," I said.

"That's too much," he said. "We'll give you thirty."

"I'll take it," I said.

I reached into my satchel and pulled out one of Mr. Woolworth's cheap felt banners. I carefully wrapped it in a newspaper and handed it to the Lima manager. He handed me the $30. He left. I left. I met the team and to-gether we headed for a street car for the railroad station.

Just as we were about to board the trolley, an angry mob came yelling after us. It was the Lima team. The manager had just told them about the deal he'd made. They weren't fooled by the banner. Since the $30 was team money, they wanted it back, every cent. I could have my banner, they said.

"Listen," I said, quaking in my boots but determined to keep a level head, "if I take back that banner, you aren't world champions any more."

That didn't stop them. I was forced to return the $30.

I put the banner back in my satchel. But from that day on, I was never without one of these banners at any game. Throughout the rest of the trip that year, I was able to sell four banners at about $50 each. What had started out as a morale booster for my team became one of the most colossal (and profitable) hoaxes I ever pulled. I continued selling the banners on every trip I took over the next ten years.

We cancelled a game at Cleveland that we were to have played after Lima. Continuing home, we arrived in Rochester at the home of Johnny Murphy on April 10. We had completed something of a record-breaking trip. Four of our players had participated in every game. Jim Murnane missed a game in Buffalo because of injuries to his ribs and another at Fort Wayne, following the first Lima battle.

The trip had been a tremendous success. I determined to give the boys a bonus. When I left Buffalo, I was in debt to them $900. By the time I got to Minneapolis, I was able to pay back some of the sum to the team. By the time we turned our steps toward Oswego, I had returned $700. By the time we reached Rochester, I had completely retired the debt and gave the boys a bonus of $100 besides.

The West was rich basketball territory. All you needed was a little reputation. But I only had five men. I had to cancel games as far out as Butte, Montana.

Never was there a more considerate and patient bunch of kids than this team. I wonder now how we managed to keep so healthy on a trip like that through all kinds of weather and taking all kinds of beatings on the way. We played night after night without rest. If one had a tooth-ache, the rest of the players would feel it. It was that kind of a team. The progress of basketball all through the West was made possible by these boys. Wherever they appeared, they made friends. It had been a great trip.

In the summer of 1914 I went to Oswego to meet Dr. Mary Walker. Mary was eighty-three years old at the time. Charles P. Gilmore, manager of the Oswego Hippodrome, and H. J. Smith of Pathe Films went with me. We drove up in my car "The Yellow Dragon." I wanted to get her to appear at the Hippodrome. Mary was a pioneer suffragette. She was also a great crusader against the use of tobacco.

I was warned never to light up a cigarette in her presence lest she hit me over the head with her umbrella. She met us at the front door of her house and insisted on stepping outside. She had on her usual man's full-dress suit, top hat, and felt boots. (She was the only woman allowed to wear men's clothing by consent of the U. S. Government.)

I asked her if she would like to take a small tour with me. Quite unexpectedly she agreed. But only if the tour was for informing mothers and fathers of young boys of the danger of smoking the "filthy weed," as she called tobacco. She also believed that if women wore men's clothes, life's evils would disappear. She claimed that the greatest sorrows that women suffered were those physical and mental ones caused by their unhygienic manner of dressing. The lack of the ballot was minor in comparison. One reform she did accomplish (which alone should have brought her fame) was in having a neckband placed between one's collar button and one's neck. This eliminated much unnecessary chafing.

Mary Walker graduated from Syracuse Medical College as an M.D. in 1855. During the Civil War, Mary was a surgeon at the front. She had the rank of first lieutenant. She wore ordinary officers' uniforms and rendered valiant service. She was taken prisoner and was exchanged for a Confederate officer. Following the war, Congress voted her a medal and gave her the right to wear men's clothing.

The first engagement I arranged for her was at the opening of the Quirk Theater in Fulton, N. Y. The "act" went like this: As she lectured the audience on the dangers of the "filthy weed," Harold Perry and his wife, star tango dancers, did their routine next to her on the stage.

"This," triumphantly declared Dr. Walker, "is what young people can accomplish if they do not use the filthy weed." The audience loved it. They applauded long and loud.

Backstage I was sneaking a smoke during her talk. As she came back, wondering if she had pleased the crowd, she saw my cigarette and stopped in horror. Then she yanked the cigarette out of my mouth. I decided I would have to give up smoking or the Doctor. I gave up the Doctor. . . . Six years later I gave up the "filthy weed."

CHAPTER NINE

THE CORNSTARCH QUINTET

ON CHRISTMAS DAY, 1914, I got married, spent one day on a honeymoon, and shipped off the next day for Erie, Pa., where I met the new season's team. It all happened like this:

I had met a girl in New York, Miss Rose Rothblum. She fell in love with the Hudson racer. We decided to get married. We set out to locate Rabbi Brodie in Syracuse.

The Rabbi told us we would need witnesses; so I stepped outside in the cold and hailed the first couple that came down Harrison Street. "Will you stand up with me while I get married?" I asked them. Although a little surprised by the sudden proposal, they agreed. I think they were more nervous than Rose and I.

We spent our honeymoon in Oswego with my sister and brother-in-law, Mr. and Mrs. Walter A. White. The next day, Rose left for New York City to stay with her mother. I left for Erie to travel with the team. Thus did I become a married man.

I have often been asked which of the many teams I managed in over thirty years of basketball was the best. Well, it's a hard question to answer. After all, some of the greatest stars in basketball history played at one time or another on my teams. Central New York has produced hundreds of accomplished athletes. Actually, I considered a number of teams my "best." One of the best, known throughout the West as the "Cornstarch Quintet," was the one I took on tour in 1914–15 after I got married.

Of course, in other years I had some greater individual stars. But stars don't always make a winning team. This year of 1915 was to be the most successful thus far in my career. The team was built around my old faithfuls Mike Roberts, Johnny Murphy, and the team captain, James Murnane. That year, too, I talked Swede Grimstead into coming West with me. That gave me the greatest center in basketball at the time, since Ed Wachter of Troy was about ready to retire.

Then there was Blubs Alberding, another old friend who had played with me at Oswego in 1912–13. Blubs had been playing in the New York State League since then and had made an excellent record as one of the best set shots in the League.

Finally, I secured the services of Jack Nolls, star of the Troy team and at the time probably the outstanding all-around player in the country. Jack was only five feet, ten; but he could outjump all the giant centers going. He had an uncanny sense of timing. He could spring at just the right moment to meet the ball before the other player touched it. He was superb on both defense and offense and a fine shot. And, for all his stocky build, he was fast. Jack was always in condition. At sixty-five, Jack was giving swimming lessons at Miami Beach.

He played five seasons with the Globe Trotters. He could save more money on these trips than even I could. He always made me pay all his traveling expenses in advance. Then on the road he would trade his charms for meals. Many an unsuspecting Midwestern lass gave Jack his supper. He was the best piano player I ever signed to a team. For that reason, Jack was popular at the dancing and parties after the games. Jack was from St. Johnsville, New York.

The team was first assembled in Dolgeville, N. Y., on November 8, 1914. Astonishingly, the players agreed to play all the games I could arrange. This included besides games in New York, Pennsylvania, and the Midwest, a chance to participate in the A.A.U. tournament in San Francisco, run in connection with the Panama Exposition. Other games were tentatively scheduled in Oregon.

The summer before, I had determined to make all future trips as comfortable and efficient as possible. I studied all the angles of hotel accommodations, conflicting dates, train connections, probable weather conditions, the matter of guarantees, probable size of crowds at each game, and so forth. For this I was later rewarded. The 1914–15 trip was a big success financially.

While waiting for the basketball months to come up on the calendar, I promoted motorcycle races at the Herkimer Fair Grounds. On Sundays I played baseball with the Herkimer Nationals, a pretty good semipro outfit. In those days, local sports had a bigger and better following than they do now.

By November 1, I had arranged 68 games, of which 36 were booked in New York and Pennsylvania. By the time the team reached Erie, Pa., I had jacked that total up to 80.

So I went off to get married and the team went off to play basketball. Jim Murnane managed affairs until I joined the group.

That year I was asked to bring my stars to Rochester to inaugurate professional basketball in The Flower City.

After playing 39 games without a defeat, we headed for Rochester to become (for awhile) the Company A team. I was determined to stay no longer than the first week in February, no matter how well the experiment went.

Our first game was against the Utica Celtics. Attendance was good. The Rochester newspapers gave the inauguration a big play. The question "Is Rochester Ready for Professional Basketball?" was bannered. People were aroused. They saw a good game, with our team beating the Celtics 51–25, even though they had such stars as Don and Ray Grant and Fay Inman.

The preliminary game was a bit unusual. The Kodak Park team played the Andrews. The Andrews were all Jewish boys. Their manager did not allow them to talk anything but Yiddish while playing. Since few other teams could understand them, he considered their "foreign language" a great advantage.

By the time we had played our second game with the Kingstons of the Hudson River League, I could see the fans weren't rallying as had been expected. We won again, 33–21. But there were only 300 present. The people were more interested in the local high school and the University of Rochester games. The Armory was too expensive to operate. I decided to continue West and let someone else "grow up" with basketball in Rochester.

The sport resumed in Rochester in 1917. It continued during the war under the leadership of Jack Neiman. In 1920–21 Neiman and old Globe Trotter Johnny Murphy joined forces to promote the game. When the American League was formed, Rochester was on the roster. From time to time various cities came in and dropped out of the League. So with Rochester. The League disbanded and reorganized in 1933–34. Rochester was not represented. Murphy and Neiman formed an independent team. Then the next year Les Harrison organized the Seegrams. Les has been in Rochester basketball ever since.

In 1937 the New York State League was organized. I was president. Harrison would not join, preferring to play independently. After the war, Harrison built a great team around Al Cervi, Bobby Davies, Red Holzman, Otto Graham, and Fuzzy LeVine. With this outfit he entered the National League as the Rochester Royals.

A basketball tournament had been set for February in Minneapolis which would bring together half a dozen of the most famous teams of the East and West. They would play for the "Championship of the United States" and were sponsored by the Minneapolis National Guard Athletic Association. The teams that would compete were Billings, Montana; Aberdeen, S. D.; Red Wing, Minn.; Fond du Lac, Wis.; and the Globe Trotters.

The tournament was to be the biggest ever staged in that part of the country. It suggested itself to the National Guardsmen when it was learned that the famous Billings team would make an Eastern trip and that the Oswego champions would make a Western trip. Perfect, they said. Why not match them with the best we have around Minneapolis?

The Five B's of Billings had been Western champions the year before. Aberdeen had won 34 out of 38 games. Fond du Lac was a known quantity of speed and basketball prowess, and Red Wing was having a basketball boom that promised to bring it right up into first class competition. Minneapolis was to pick an all-star team from its local sixteen-team National Guard League and send them against the visiting squads. Ascension, St. Joe, and University stars were available.

So we set our course for Minneapolis. Our schedule had been planned so that we would arrive in time for the important tournament.

In Detroit we met our first defeat of the trip. We played the Rayls in the Moose Temple there on a Friday night. That was a Friday night that the team and I didn't soon forget. About every rule ever contemplated by either the A.A.U., the Intercollegiate Association, James Naismith, or Lambert Will was broken that night.

The Rayls upset the laws of the game more effectively than we. They won 23–17. The game was described by local sportswriters in the Detroit *News* as the roughest played on a Detroit court in years. Their foul shooting decided the contest. Runkle of Detroit made 10 out of 18 throws. We made only 3 out of 14 chances.

For the first few minutes of the game, the Rayls rode Murnane and Nolls out of the court every time they came near the basket. In self-defense, we began to fight back. Then it turned into a football game, with tripping, clipping, charging, hipping, and riding.

This was, however, almost typical of the basketball of that time. It was a man's game. It wasn't bogged down with picayune fouls, tyrannical officials, and tall, clumsy players. Though the Detroit game was an extreme instance of rough play, it was also the kind of game that kept crowd interest high and competitive spirits flaming.

Every once in a while, we would run up against some local team that was so fired up with the prospect of beating the "World Champions" that they beat us with sheer emotional frenzy. They went at us in the same spirit that teams nowadays go after Notre Dame. Everyone wanted to pin up one of my championship banners in their Athletic Club.

Did you ever dream that you had performed some

heroic deed and were coming home to a great welcome? That's about the way we felt when our train pulled into Toledo. A large crowd, including many lovely girls, was waiting to greet us on the platform. I decided I was as popular as Admiral Dewey. News of my prowess in Fort Wayne must certainly have reached Toledo!

Modest soul that I was, I turned to the boys and said, "This celebration must be for Willis Knight."

Mr. Knight, who engineered the Overland automobile, was on our train. He had just invented a new fastener to hold auto curtains together. The side curtains on the Overland would now be equipped with overshoe buckles instead of buttons.

But no one paid any attention to Willis Knight when he stepped off the train. They were waiting for us. The mob came for us, yelling, "You bunch of dirty scabs!" They pushed and shoved, waving the signs they carried, yelling and screaming.

We ran for the station with the crowd behind us, still in the dark as to why they were so mad at us. "Scab" meant nothing to us. We dashed through the station and out onto the street in search of a cab. Some of the crowd began to throw stones and bricks. We ducked the Irish confetti as best as we could while the cab driver whipped his bay horse into a gallop just ahead of the cascade of stones and brickbats. The signs read "The Management Is Unfair," and "Keep your Weight Down. Eat in the Next Town," and "Don't Bite the Hand That's Feeding You." They only mystified us all the more.

The cab stopped suddenly in the middle of Toledo's main street, but the crowd hadn't given up the chase. They closed in again and began pushing us around. Not a cop in sight. We didn't know what to do. Some of the women reached into the cab and dragged out our suit-

cases, ripping them open. All the time they were screaming in our faces, "Scab, scab!" We were accused of trying
to take away their bread and butter. Mike Roberts tried
to tell one of the rioters that we were merely basketball
players from New York.

Most of the crowd roared at us again. They didn't
believe it. But they could find nothing in our suitcases
to disprove it. They accused us of invading Toledo to
break their strike for more pay and shorter hours. Mike
insisted we would rather live on pumpernickle and lard
than take away their bread and butter. We tried to tell
them we were the Oswego World Champions.

By this time, some two thousand people had gathered
in the street. The crowd was in an angry mood. The
non-strikers were sympathetic with the strikers. Our position was precarious. With the slightest provocation they
would have beaten and trampled us to a pulp.

Luckily, someone in the crowd, heeding our pleas that
we were basketball players, produced an evening paper
in which our pictures appeared. It was a lucky break. This
convinced the crowd that we were harmless. I immediately
wrote out a pass for that night's game and gave it to the
man who had saved our hides. The strikers were still in
an angry mood, however. We hopped back into the cab
and got out of there fast.

By the time we had finished dinner that night and had
settled down in the YMCA, we were pretty tired. We told
the room clerk what had happened. He already knew the
whole story. It seems the president of the waiters' union
in Cleveland had seen us take the noon train from there
to Toledo. He wired the waiters' headquarters in Toledo
that six or seven Cleveland waiters had left for Toledo
to take jobs away from Toledo strikers.

Later a committee of the strikers sought us out and apologized. They said the joke was on the Toledo waiters. Some joke—almost trampled to death!

We lost the game with Toledo and journeyed on to Cleveland, where we lost again. That made 3 straight losses after winning 41 in a row. We had that big Minneapolis tournament coming up; so I cautioned the boys to take it easy. After the roughing we had received in Detroit, I didn't want anyone to get hurt and have to drop out of the lineup. In Cleveland it was the Broadway Y team and its captain, Bill Schardt, that beat us. Schardt, by the way, was a Brooklyn Dodger, one of the best pitchers of that day.

Following Cleveland, we boarded the train for Lima and there got back on the winning side again. The White Stars weren't up to the team of 1914. We took them 30–8 in another rough and tumble affair, blanking them in the first half.

The local paper said it was no disgrace to be beaten by us "No, indeed! No alibi is needed when a team not of championship caliber ties into the Oswego crowd. The champs are basketball players—and finished athletes, too —rough 'em up style, or any old style. At the rough style, Forward Murphy towers above the whole gang as a star. He can rough a whole team at one time and not know that he is exerting himself.

"With Murphy in the lineup, the Oswego soldiers look the part of a hard-traveling, seasoned outfit capable of engaging a German regiment in open battle. At times the Oswegos made the locals look foolish with their passwork and team play, and near the finish delighted themselves by toying with the Limaites at intervals."

Following Lima came a victory at For Wayne over the Knights of Columbus team. From there we went to Chicago, and for a time I thought that would be our last stop in this world. I had engaged to play the Mercury Athletic Club there. Mercury is a harmless-sounding name. No one would have reason to suspect a club called that. Two games were to be played, one Sunday evening, one Monday.

Advance instructions were to stop at the Jackson Hotel. Here we had our first glimpse of what lay ahead. All kinds of underworld characters loafed and lounged around the lobby. The place was a hangout for worn-out wrestlers and pugs, some with cauliflower ears and broken noses. It sent the chills up our backs to see these toughs give us the eye as we signed up. We were to play our games in, of all places, Hull House! Poor Jane Addams never realized what sort of people would inhabit her project in later years. As we left the Jackson Hotel, something made me feel I never should have booked those two games. The basketball court was located on the fourth floor. Before the game someone told us that two murders had been committed there just recently.

The games, of course, were advertised as being for the "World Championship." I was somewhat encouraged when I learned that William "Big Bill" Thompson, Republican Mayor of the city, and Robert M. Switzer, Democratic candidate for the office, were to be guests. Knowing nothing of Chicago or of the politics there, I supposed the presence of these two public servants would keep such characters as we had seen at the Jackson Hotel in line. "Big Bill" (he weighed better than 300) was to toss the ball up to begin the game. Switzer would make the next tossup.

Play commenced. The crowd contained assorted groups of rough-looking fellows who began to taunt and jeer us in language that shocked even our hardened ears. That wasn't all. The game wasn't two minutes old before Jack

Nolls was hit over the eye with a cud of chewing tobacco thrown from the balcony. This was a warning of what was to come. The Mercurys bore down, taking advantage of our confusion and "fouling out" a victory, 28–23.

Between halves, I decided I wanted to get out of my deal just as fast as I could. Although I had engaged to play another game with the Mercurys, I knew after that first half that I could never allow my team to meet such a bunch of hoodlums again. I went outside and telephoned Belvidere, Ill., whose team had been anxious to play us. They agreed to a game two nights later, the date of our second game with the Mercurys.

The finish of the Mercury game came after forty minutes of threats and abuse. When I approached the manager for our guarantee of $125, he and his gang were so ugly that I was scared to count the money when he handed it to me. Later, when I did count it, I had only $58. But I was mighty glad to get that and get out alive.

I announced that we were canceling our second game. That was a mistake! We kept moving toward the basement, followed by a mob yelling at us to "get out fast if you know what's good for you!"

We finally landed in the boiler room and there found a savior in a big-shouldered Irishman who happened to be the fireman as well as relief janitor. He picked up a heavy crow bar and took up a station at the door. Then he yelled out at the pursuing Mercury crowd, "Come on, you dirty bums, I'll throw ye in the furnace."

No one opened that door.

"I know that gang," he said. "They probably gave you a little money for playing and now they want to take it away from you."

We were safe enough for the moment, but how were we to get our clothes and get out of Hull House? The kindly Irishman solved it. He went outside (well-armed) and telephoned the police. Soon two plain-clothesmen came over and escorted us to our clothes and then out of the building.

"Where are you boys staying?" they asked.

"At the Jackson Hotel," we answered.

"Oh, no," they said. "You're not staying there. Not unless you want us to carry you out in boxes tomorrow morning."

We didn't want that very much; so we let them take us to the Morrison Hotel.

Before we left we tried to tip the good janitor. "Nothing doing," he said, "I got children of me own. Good luck to you boys!"

I tried to get him to write down his name and address, but he could neither read nor write. I have since lost trace of him. He was certainly a Godsend that night.

The policemen took us to our door at the Morrison Hotel. "Go to bed and spend tomorrow around this section of the city. You will like it. Nobody knows you here," they advised us. They didn't want us to leave Chicago with the idea that the whole city was made up of Jackson Hotels and Hull Houses.

We had no sooner entered the hotel than I heard myself being paged over the loud speaker. It was a telegram from Princeton (Wisconsin) wanting to know if we had any open dates, but I was frightened before I found out why my name was being called. How did anyone know we were here? Had the Mercury crowd followed us in spite of the police? Were they even then preparing to trap us? As it developed, the two policemen had checked us out of the Jackson Hotel. Our stuff was taken to the Morrison. I plopped into a chair for a breather.

"Well, that's over," I exclaimed. "Let's have a little game of cards and relax."

The team thought that was a good idea so off we went to the elevator to go to our rooms. As we entered the elevator, I noticed two men in the hotel lobby watching us. They came up with us and followed us halfway down our hall. We were suspicious, but with six of us in the gang we felt we could handle the two if they started trouble. We got to our room and locked the door.

Grimstead dug out the cards and we pulled up chairs and started to play. Just then there was a sharp rap, rap on the door.

I looked at Grimstead and he looked at me. We were all scared.

"Who's there?" I finally managed to squeak out.

"House detectives," came the reply.

Like hell, I thought. It's probably some of the Mercury boys come to collect that $58.

"Boys, don't pull any funny stuff in there. This is a new and respectable hotel and it's absolutely against the policy of the hotel to allow any gambling."

We still thought it was a put-up job, but finally we became convinced that they really were house detectives. We let them in, showed them our championship banners, and explained who we were. I showed them the telegram I had just received from Princeton. Apparently assured that we were all right, they left.

I went downstairs to call Princeton. The detectives were still hanging around in the hall. They followed me to the lobby. They wanted to know where I was going.

"To use the telephone," I replied.

"Why don't you use the telephone in your room?" they wanted to know.

"Because I don't want the boys to hear what I'm going to say."

"Why don't you want them to hear?" they asked.

Well, it wasn't any of their business why, but I didn't want to antagonize them, so I told them why. "Because the boys expect a vacation now that we don't have to play here again tomorrow and I'm now going to arrange for another game instead."

Talk about suspicious cops! They still weren't convinced. They followed me to the phone. I called Princeton and let them listen in. I said to the Princeton manager, "The only open date we have is tomorrow."

The Princeton manager replied, "Let me think. Would you come for one hundred?"

"Make it one hundred and twenty-five and the World Champions will be there tomorow."

The manager agreed. One detective turned to the other. "Only one day's notice and he's got a game. This guy is a real champ." Then he turned to me and apologized for their suspicions. They wished us good luck.

When I got back to the room, I found the boys were planning to do a little shopping in Chicago the next day. "I'm sorry, boys. We leave for Princeton in the morning. We're going back to college," I said, trying to be funny. There was no response. Nobody said good night to me that night.

In the early days of basketball, games between professional and collegiate teams were common. The Buffalo Germans frequently played college teams. The same was true of the 23rd Street Y and the Washington Continentals of Schenectady.

In 1915, when Union College ruled the small college basketball world and Schenectady's professionals captured the championship of the New York State League, there were many debates among Schenectady fans as to which was the better team. To settle the argument, the teams played an exhibition game in the Schenectady Armory at the close of the college's season. The pros won.

At the turn of the century, Syracuse University was a member of a City League which included the Syracuse Y, Syracuse Athletic Association, and the Athletic Club. A feud between the University and the Y resulted in the break-up of the league. The two teams wound up one of their games in a tie. Under the rules then, if teams were tied after the regulation playing time, play was to be resumed until one team scored a goal—the "sudden death" rule.

In that particular game the University squad refused to play off the tie and the contest was forfeited to the Y. The next day the University withdrew from the league. With only three teams left, the league decided it was inadvisable to continue and disbanded.

After Princeton, we went on to Belvidere, Ill. The town was ready for us. With only the shortest possible notice, the forthcoming game had been advertised all over the town and surrounding countryside. Everyone talked about the game and the Globe Trotters—and winning the World Championship.

I was pleased that we had arrived in this beautiful city early in the afternoon. We promenaded up and down Main Street giving the town the once over. The people promenaded up and down with us, giving us the once over. It was excellent publicity.

A complete sellout featured the game that night. People were turned away at the doors. The game was hard and cleanly fought. We won 28–21. The fine people of Belvidere were loyal fans and the treatment we received was in startling contrast to the experience we had just been through in the Windy City. The young ladies, I remember, were exceptionally nice during the customary after-game dancing.

We kept going night after night until we arrived for our first series of the year with Fond du Lac. The fans there were confident their team could repeat last year's performance and beat us again. They were in for a surprise. They were amazed with the performance of Swede Grimstead, Jack Nolls, and Blubs Alberding. We gained a great many supporters during that series when we beat little Fondy two games straight.

The last day in Fond du Lac, as we were preparing to continue our journey toward the Coast, the United States Marshal who operated the hotel where we were staying, offered to let us run the establishment during that afternoon. So for two hours the Basloe Globe Trotters became the Basloe Lobby Trotters. The joke proved to be a good publicity stunt. Hundreds of people in that little city had a grand time walking through the hotel and getting served by the champions themselves. Swede was bell hop, Nolls was elevator boy, Mike was desk clerk, Blubs was janitor and bus boy. Murphy was chef and Murnane was manager. We had a—oh, yes, I was chambermaid—grand time. It was good to break the routine of one-night stands with little time-out for pleasure. To this day I still make the beds in my house every morning before leaving for my office. My wife may not have had her husband around for a honeymoon that year, but at least he learned how to make beds while he was gone.

We moved on to Neenah-Menasha, Appleton, Green Bay, and Milwaukee. From there we moved to Minnesota where, almost as in 1914, we played two games against the Ascension team of Minneapolis, two games against the St. Joseph team of St. Paul, one game against Company D of Minneapolis, two games at Red Wing, and one game against the excellent Chaska outfit.

We took first honors in the Minenapolis series, beating St. Joseph 29–13. But we ran into trouble the next night against the Ascension team. Less than a minute after the game began, their big center made a basket. They were never headed after that. The next night we played the Ascensions again. This time some trouble developed. The referee didn't like rough language.

"If you use any improper language, I shall blow my whistle immediately," he warned before we began.

Five minutes later he called a foul on Johnny Murphy for running with the ball. Murphy lost his temper. He wanted to know what the foul was all about. The referee said it was for traveling.

"Traveling where?" Murphy inquired.

The referee put Johnny out of the game. Murphy lost his temper and knocked the referee's whistle out of his hand. Jim Murnane, standing nearby, gave the whistle a kick that sent it the length of the playing floor. The crowd came to its feet. Boos and catcalls echoed through the hall. A couple of spectators got off the benches and started toward the players in the center of the floor. A riot threatened.

I rushed from my seat and began talking—fast. "Let's not get excited," I pleaded. "No harm meant here. Go back to your seats. The boys were just having a little fun."

I collared Johnny and steered him off the floor. The players on the other team helped keep the spectators from starting to fight. The referee finally restored order. The crowd resumed their seats. The boos quieted down. The toss up was made and the game continued. On the bench, Johnny Murphy used some hard words on that referee.

I was visiting with some of the spectators—the cool ones

—after the game. One seemed to know local history. Since I was anxious to learn how Minneapolis got its name, I asked him. According to this man, a Colonel John H. Stevens filed a claim to a large section of downtown Minneapolis in 1849. It was laid out as a town in 1854. The name "Minneapolis" was suggested by a man named Charles Hoag in 1852. It was a combination of "Minnehaha" (Laughing Waters) and the Greek word "Polis," meaning city.

When he finished his story, an old man of about seventy came up and joined the conversation. "I hear yer story," he said with a broad Swedish accent. "And I tank Minneapolis ban named after woman called "Minnie.""

The first man looked at him in some surprise. But we didn't see the joke. Grimstead, the Swede, bit. "How did they get the appolis?" he asked.

"Minnie, she ban like apples."

Next stop was Bemidji, Minnesota. It was a tiring train ride. We dragged into the hotel grimy and mussed. Before supper we took scrub baths. Then down to eat. Sitting in the beautiful old-fashioned dining room were four very handsome young ladies. We had seen nothing so nice on the trip.

"You take the dining room, I'll take the girls," said Johnny Murphy.

They were all in one corner as though they were holding a meeting. But we could see they were watching us. We walked in rather noisily just to make sure they wouldn't miss us. We headed for the seats next to them, but being gentlemen, didn't attempt to speak to them.

We immediately were aware that they were not speaking English. I could speak five languages, and I recognized their speech as Polish. Of course, they did not know one of us could understand them. They were making comments on the five noisy boys who had just entered the dining room.

"I think he's the most handsome," said one of them, indicating Jim Murnane. Personally, I thought Jim the homeliest man on the team. I didn't profess to be a Rudolph Valentino, but I wasn't the worst looking guy in the bunch. They thought Mike Roberts a friendly boy. But he didn't appeal to them. Grimstead was good-looking, but his teeth were too big. Jack Nolls was "cock-eyed" and Alberding had a "foolish laugh."

Supper was not yet being served; so before they could get around to me, I decided to give Nature a hand. I went back upstairs. The others were surprised to see me leave without an explanation. Back in our room, I shaved, re-scrubbed my face and hands, polished my shoes, and combed my hair with lots of vaseline. Then I returned. The girls were still there talking. So was the team. Neither had talked to the other as yet. I sat down and listened hard for comment.

"His feet are too big," said one girl. The rest agreed.

After all the trouble I had gone to, they still thought Murnane was the best-looking. This was a blow to my vanity. Suppertime arrived. We took our places at the table. The girls began waiting on us. As the one who had thought my feet too big came up to me, I spoke to her in Polish. Her mouth dropped open in surprise. The other girls stopped what they were doing. Then in their confusion and betrayal they all rushed for the kitchen. Their cheeks were flaming. It wasn't long before the proprietor came out, his face red from the stew kettle over which he'd been working.

"What's the trouble out here?" he demanded. "One of you guys been nasty and insulted my girls?"

"On the contrary," I said, "they've insulted me." Then

I switched languages and addressed him in Polish. He understood. I told him of the conversation, of the estimation in which the girls held me, and of the fact that I paid the team's bill and would appreciate his support. Then back to English: "Who do you think is the best looking?" I demanded.

"I'm looking at him," said the proprietor. The girls said no more. I sat down satisfied. Of course, I couldn't go out with any of those waitresses later. I was a married man.

After the completion of the grueling Minneapolis series, we were ready to head West. On a Sunday morning in February, I made arrangements to take the "Flour Special" to San Francisco. It was called that because the milling association of Minneapolis had chartered it to take their delegates to a Frisco convention. They allowed us a 50 per cent reduction on our tickets.

On the train we found a great many flour executives. Grimstead led the way to the luxurious club car where the big men were puffing away on expensive cigars and sipping highballs. Swede ordered his usual beer. Alberding and Roberts didn't order anything for fear I would make them pay for it. I was worried because the team wanted to be just as rich-acting as the flour men—and that was impossible on my expense account.

Somehow I knew our trip would be cut short. It was too good. I may be superstitious, but I felt something like a premonition of what was going to happen. Everyone on the team was making big plans for the Coast.

Sure enough, we hadn't spent one night on the train when it happened. Just as we were entering the state of Montana the red cap came through yelling my name. "Telegram for Mr. Frank Basloe." The news wasn't as good as it had been the last time I was paged in Chicago.

I could have my telegram at the next station he said. That was Butte. I secured my telegram. Everyone crowded around curiously. I read the message.

"Well, boys, we now leave the Flour Special."

"What for? What's happened, Frank?"

"We've been barred from the tournament," I said. "This note says it's because we played for money on our way out here. So we aren't amateurs any more and can't play in the A.A.U. Series."

"What do you mean?" Swede wanted to know.

"They mean you have no right to accept money for playing," I answered him bitterly.

The team was surely disappointed. They had been set not only on seeing the Coast, but also on winning that tournament.

(We heard later that Fond du Lac, a Minneapolis team, and Toledo also had been barred from the tournament for the same reason. That made us feel better. In fact, the players reasoned that they were probably in a higher class than mere "amateurs.")

We went back onto the train and explained to the milling executives that we could go no farther with them. But in spite of the news, they wanted us to continue on with them to San Francisco. They said they would intercede for us when we got to the Coast and possibly their influence might change the minds of the tournament officials.

The train stayed in Butte for half an hour. There was a great commotion on the train. Everyone tried to talk us into going West. They were real friends. When I finally convinced them that it was useless to continue the trip, they set about taking up a collection to help finance the loss we would be forced to take.

"Gentlemen," I said, very touched with their consideration, "we can't take your money. Remember, that would make us professionals."

This brought a real laugh and cheered up the crowd. The conductor signalled to the engineer to be on his way and the "Flour Special" slowly clicked out of Butte. We waved for as long as the train was visible.

How quickly our rosy picture of affluence was changed to one of near poverty! While on the train and in the fancy club car, the team had enjoyed the limit in luxury. Now, standing on the wind-chilled train platform in Butte with the temperature below zero, they were stunned.

It didn't take me long to decide what our course must be. Games that far west would be scarce. We would never make a living playing in Montana. We must head back east toward the basketball haven of Minnesota and Wisconsin. In less than an hour, with the help of more than fifty telegrams, I had ten games booked. I even found a few teams in Montana willing to play us.

In less than a week we were off again. This time our train headed east. First stop was Bismarck, North Dakota. As an added attraction in Bismarck, I decided to advertise Mike Roberts as the world's greatest foul shooter. We got such good advance publicity on this from the local papers that by game time the auditorium was filled to capacity.

Both teams walked out onto the playing court. After practice, Mike advanced to the foul line with the grace of a ballet dancer. The referee held up his hand. The crowd fell silent.

"Introducing Mike Roberts, the world's greatest foul shooter!"

Mike took a bow. The referee handed him the ball. There wasn't a sound in the hall as Mike turned to face the basket. Holding the ball easily he bent, swung back and forth twice, and then lofted the ball to the basket.

It bounced on the rim once, twice—and then fell away. There was a slight murmur of surprise from the crowd. The referee picked up the ball and handed it to Mike again.

Once more Mike took the ball in his hands like an expert, wound up, tossed—and missed. The spectators began to turn in surprise and vexation to their neighbors with silent but meaningful looks. Mike continued. The ball just wouldn't go into the basket. Out of fifteen, poor Mike missed thirteen.

Someone in the audience yelled, "Hey, you bum, you couldn't hit a bushel basket!" Then the whole crowd began booing and hissing and stamping its feet, howling that we were fakes.

At last the game began. The referee was a local man and, of course, he wanted to be very fair. After seeing Mike's foul shooting, he was sure he could call unlimited fouls against the home team and not hurt their chances. So he called 15 on them. But Mike fooled him. He made 14 of those 15 shots, much to the dismay of the Bismarck players. We won 47–17. The fans all believed Mike had missed the earlier baskets on purpose. But that wasn't so. Mike always tried hard.

Incidentally, Mike wasn't feeling very well at that time. That afternoon before the game I had taken him to one of the local doctors. After an examination, the doctor said, "Young man, you should stop smoking. You should also stop drinking. And above all, don't go out with any of these wild women in the West, especially while you're playing basketball."

Mike was peeved. "Come on, Frank, let's get out of here," he said, getting up from the chair. "This guy is crazy. He wants me to stop living." We left, slamming the door behind us.

From Bismarck, we shipped off for Duluth, Minnesota. There I made arrangements for my team to play the winner in the finals for the National Championship. As it turned out, Fond du Lac won the championship and we agreed to meet in a three-game series in February, 1915, for the championship of the East and West. We got a good guarantee. The winner of the event would get 75 per cent of the receipts. Every man was anxious to take the important series with Fond du Lac. This would mark us as champions for sure.

As was usual with us, we played every night we could get a game. Although there was a championship series beginning Thursday of that week, we scheduled games for Monday, Tuesday, and Wednesday. On the first day, we played Two Harbors, then Pine River, and finally on Wednesday the Bemidji team.

The Pine River expedition was an unusual one—even for us. There were only a hotel, drug store, school, grocery store, and a few houses in the town. There were some very distinguished-looking men staying at the hotel with us. One of them was a prosperous lumber dealer and a former Yale football star by the name of Shevlin. He was putting on the game for the benefit of his friends. We were getting $200 guaranteed.

The game was to be played in one of the school rooms. They expected forty people at a dollar apiece. I couldn't figure out where the other $160 was coming from. I hoped I wouldn't have to take it in cord wood.

At the schoolhouse, we found that the playing floor wasn't much larger than the barn in which I used to play back in Herkimer. It would hold no more than forty spectators.

I was standing at the door next to the ticket seller when spectator No. 39 walked in and paid his dollar. Just then, the basketball got away from the players practicing on the floor and bounced under the bleachers. The fellow at the door who was taking tickets and visiting with me asked me to watch the door while he went under the bleachers to get the ball. As he did, spectator No. 40 came in, handed me a silver dollar, and took his seat.

When the door tender returned, he asked, "Did someone come in while I was under the bleachers?"

I said jokingly, "Not a soul."

He wasn't convinced. "By gosh, that's funny. I thought I heard someone coming in through the door while I was crawling under the bleachers."

"I don't know where he could have gone," I said. The doorkeeper insisted Spectator No. 40 must be there. Thereupon he closed the door and started to count the people in the audience. He counted forty. Then he asked me to count. I counted thirty-nine. This continued for about five minutes. Finally the harried ticket taker called over another man and asked him to count the spectators. He counted forty. I asked them if they issued any free passes.

"No. Everyone has to pay to get in here regardless of who they are," he answered angrily.

The game, held up until then, was started. The matter of Spectator No. 40 was dropped. We won 19–9.

After the game, I received a check for $199 from the druggist and treasurer. He asked me if the amount was suitable.

"There is some mistake," I said. "This check is for $199 and our guarantee was for $200."

"Yes, I know," said the druggist. "You took tickets while the secretary went under the bleachers for the ball.

And I happen to be the man who was No. 40 and who gave you a silver dollar when I came through the door."

In the first of the big championship battles George Fogarty of Fondy turned what looked like a tie game into a victory for the Wisconsin lads by making a basket in the last ten seconds of play. The final score was 26–24.

Friday, the story was different. Despite a treacherously slippery playing floor, we downed them 30–26. Mike Roberts' shooting in this game, unlike his "foul" exhibition in Bismarck, was superb. With three minutes to play, the score was again tied. Then we came through with two baskets and the game was ours. That evened the series. Everything depended on the final game the following night, Saturday.

The team came through. About 2100 people in the Duluth Armory saw Fond du Lac tumble from their pedestal by 26–17. We outplayed the Fondy team throughout the game. It seemed we couldn't miss that night. There was a lot of rough play, but they didn't have the old fire they had had the year before.

A great many people who live east of Milwaukee have never seen an Indian. The only Indians I knew were those about whom I had read stories. However, on two or three occasions during our tour of the West in 1915 we met and played against real Indian basketball teams.

I had always been told the Indians were easy to cheat out of their land. I was sure I would have no trouble dealing with them. My first experience was at Odanah, Wis., and I learned a lesson. When we arrived, I was told how to get to the reservation. Imagine our astonishment when we found that the manager was a real Wild West Indian chief with beautiful black hair and scanty beard. He had small black eyes with high cheek bones, a narrow forehead, and reddish brown, almost cinnamon complexion.

The chief directed us to our rooms over the commissary, a building that would cover almost half a city block. On its second floor was the basketball court.

Some of us visited the school and found some of the Indians not only spoke good English, but were well educated as well.

After an excellent lunch that day, we were invited to the home of two young ladies. To this day I remember them as two of the most beautiful girls I ever met. We spent the afternoon in their home—hoping no young Indians would call. The girls told us about Indian history. One thing they told us was that years ago Indian girls danced alone. That night after the game we were mighty glad the custom had changed.

The game was a surprise to me. The physical prowess of the Indians was almost unbelievable. All the boys were nearly six feet. They started out running at top speed and never stopped. We had never seen such speed and endurance.

We let them run while we played a waiting game. Unlike modern relay-race basketball, the sport then required some skill. The Indians' speed did not make them better basketball players. We won 38–22. It was a great sight to see so many Indians in full regalia at the game.

When it came time for the payment of our guarantee, the manager and a couple of associates came over and the chief started to count out the money. He looked at me as he might have looked at General Custer. I was just a bit nervous. He smoked his pipe and I smoked my pipe. He counted out $90. We were supposed to get $135.

The chief said, "You get $45 tomorrow morning when you wake up."

To save trouble, I agreed. I didn't close my eyes all night waiting for morning and the $45. After breakfast at the reservation, we left for the railroad station. We saw everybody but the big chief. I was hoping he wanted to gain my confidence and put in a late appearance. My players put on an Indian dance to remind me our train was coming in, but the chief never showed up. Perhaps he was thinking of his ancestors who had been robbed of their land by the white man. He picked on the wrong guy, though. My parents and grandparents were all in Austria-Hungary when that steal was going on. I told my troubles to an Indian on the train.

He said, "Simple justice and honesty in the dealings of your ancestors would have prevented him from thinking of cheating you." Whatever the cause and the justification, I got scalped for $45.

I had another experience with an Indian. He was Tom Longboat, the famous runner. I managed him for about a month. His victory at the Polo Grounds over such stars as Alfred Schrubb, Dorando, and Johnny Hayes, the Olympic champion, was something to behold. Ten thousand people witnessed a spectacle that made marathon history.

Tom Longboat's endurance was superior to any white man's. He could run seventy or eighty miles a day. As a result of his victory, an Indian from his reservation presented him with his daughter. The agreement had been: if Tom won, he got a wife; if he didn't win, he didn't get the wife.

After the victory, I decided to head back for Herkimer until Tom's honeymoon was over. The bride's father was to remain in New York until after the honeymoon. Then he would take his daughter back to Desoronta, near

Toronto, where Longboat and his bride were eventually to make their home. Tom would then meet me in Herkimer.

I was skeptical. I doubted that I would ever see Tom Longboat again, what with his new bride and his love of "fire water."

But to my surprise he did show up in Herkimer, minus bride and father-in-law. The announcement in the local paper created a sensation. My father arranged that Longboat appear in no other place in town except his store, and we gave him the best bed in the Basloe home. Business for Papa's little store doubled that week.

We gave exhibitions in Syracuse and Utica. Schenectady was to be next, but while we stopped off for an afternoon appearance at the Opera House in Little Falls, I left him to go back to Herkimer to get some of my clothes for the tour. When I returned, I could not find Longboat, and I had to disappoint a sell-out crowd in Schenectady. I never saw or heard from him again until I recently read that he had died a street cleaner in Toronto.

Before we left Minnesota, we accomplished a feat that would dumfound modern players and promoters. We played three games in one day. It was a Saturday. The first game was at 3 P.M. against the Chisholm team, the next was at 8 P.M. against the Virginia team, and the final game was at 10 P.M. against the Hibbings team. The boys won the first game, showered, ate a light lunch, and taxied over to another gym. There they licked the Virginia team in a hard battle. Then we all jumped back into a taxi, drove over to the Hibbings gym, and won again.

In Racine, on March 29, we took on the husky Horlick's Malted Milk Co. team. They claimed the Northwestern Championship and had an excellent reputation. They didn't know their own strength on the floor. That malted milk builds big muscles, believe me!

We played two games with them—lost the first and won the second. The referee enjoyed both games—from the sidelines. He forgot he had a whistle. Once we saw that the husky Horkicks were accustomed to playing with nothing illegal, we changed our style of play and socked and tripped as much as they. Murphy turned his ankle. He tried to play with it bandaged, but finally had to go out. With five minutes left in the game, Nolls was pushed into the wall and stunned for a minute. But Jack refused to quit. Racine was his home town. (A fine way to treat a home town boy!) Then with only a minute to go, Alberding got into a scrap with one of the Malted Milk boys who slugged him in the forehead just as he was about to shoot.

Come the second game, my team as yet had no broken bones, but they had some that were badly bent. The score at the end of the first half was 22–8 in our favor and in the second 8–6 in favor of the Malted Milks. That was because I played some of the last half. The team was so badly bruised they couldn't last the whole game. Murnane came through like a champion, however. He hadn't been more than bumped in the first game; so he was able to play the whole second game. He scored 20 points. Grimstead kept the crowd in an uproar with his tactics and even crippled Alberding played a great game until he was hurt again. If there was ever any doubt that my "basketbrawlers" were champions, this game dispelled it.

After the warfare was over, we were treated to fine drinks of malted milk. The Malted Milks hadn't come out of the game without bruises, either. So, holding our hurts with one hand, we drank with the other. They wanted a third game with us. But we were booked up solid until April 15 with games in Illinois, Indiana, Ohio, and Pennsylvania; so we couldn't oblige them.

So we headed East again. In Dayton, Ohio, we stopped off to play the St. Mary Cadets team. Up to this point we had won 96 games and lost but 4 on a trip that often included hard games on successive days. (In one sequence we had played ten games in seven days.) Now we had but seven more games to play. We beat the Cadets 28–24.

In Dayton, we heard a lot about the Wright brothers and even saw an occasional flying machine go rattling overhead. We all craned our necks until they were stiff and sore watching these man-made birds. There was nothing like this in the Mohawk Valley. But one of the boys was quick to see possibilities in the contraption.

"Why don't you get one of those things and fly us around the country?" asked Johnny Murphy. . . .

At last we headed back to Herkimer. It was the greatest trip ever made by a basketball team. After Nolls and Roberts recovered from the banging they took in Racine, we would be ready to tackle anybody, anywhere, any time.

I hoped to play Troy and Carbondale for the "Championship of the World" at Carbondale. These two teams and the Globe Trotters were the three best teams in the country.

The Troy team was made up of the great Ed Wachter, Lew Wachter, Flo Haggerty, Bill Hardiman, Chief Muller, Dick Leary, Johnny Nugent, and Andy Suils. They also had taken a swing through the West. They had played Chaska and beaten them 19–18. We had beaten Chaska 18–17. Chaska, incidentally, was one of the greatest teams we met in twenty years of traveling.

When Troy returned East, they disbanded. Carbondale and the Globe Trotters set a series at Carbondale. We agreed to play the first half of the game with open baskets in the net—the style Carbondale had been using. For the second half, backboards were to be put up.

My boys had been playing with backboards. This made it difficult for us in the first half. But even so, we remained even. However, Carbondale refused after the first half to put up the backboards. We lost the game and I refused to finish the series. The affair attracted quite a little attention at the time. Carbondale had a great team, but they were no better than the Globe Trotters. On the Carbondale team was Barney Sedran, Marty Friedman, Jack Inglis, Elmer Ripley, Jack Fox, Chief Muller, Bill Hempinstall, Jim Mahon, Homeny Hubbard, Jim Daly, and James St. Ledger.

No one on my team came home starved or broke. Not only were we a playing success, but we also made money. I sold four banners as well at $50 apiece, and I gave each member of the team a $50 bonus.

We all talked about what we would do with our fortunes. Grimstead said he was going to buy better beer. Murnane, Roberts, and Murphy sent their $50 to their mothers.

CHAPTER TEN

"HOW YOU GONNA KEEP 'EM DOWN ON THE FARM . . ."

OUR BAGS REMAINED UNPACKED and gathered dust for a year, while the boys went about their hometown trades. My wife was with child and I had to think of settling down with a business. My father had built another store next door to his original venture, and he offered me a job. My salary would be $15 a week with eats and a small apartment. But the grocery business held little attraction for me.

I remembered an event back in 1905. On Halloween that year, some of the kids in the neighborhood and I had removed the front door steps from my parents' home and put them against a neighbor's house. Then we took the "For Sale" sign in front of this neighbor's house and stuck it in front of my parents' house.

The next day three prospective buyers came into my father's store and wanted to know what he wanted for his house. My father said his house was not for sale.

"Then why do you have a 'For Sale' sign in front?" they wanted to know.

Since my father couldn't read, he didn't believe in signs. But the incident made a big impression on me. If it was that easy to sell property, why not make a business of it?

The prospect of a new business excited me. It had so many possibilities that a grocery store would never have. So against the advice of my father and mother, I opened an office in the small building where my father had started his first grocery store. By the end of September, 1915, I had convinced my parents, my wife, and myself that the move had been a wise one. I have never regretted the decision in thirty-five years of selling real estate. I've kept my desk in the same little building ever since.

But by the time the leaves began to fall and wood smoke from the fires of Herkimer again sharpened the air, I grew restless in spite of my new business. Offers for games throughout New York, Pennsylvania, Ohio, Illinois, Indiana, and Wisconsin flooded into my office. My wife said O.K. to just one more trip if I would then call it quits. (She never dreamed there would be eight more.)

So I put away my deeds and contracts, closed my roll-top desk, and dug out my suitcase from the closet. It was time to start another "Globe Trotting" trip.

That season I lost the service of Swede Grimstead and Blubs Alberding. They had agreed to play with Utica in the New York State League. Jim Murnane and Jack Nolls decided to become promoters themselves. They managed the Mohawk Team in the State League.

But this didn't stop me from heading west. There were many other players around Central New York. Two of my old stalwarts, Mike Roberts and Johnny Murphy, although they had received many excellent offers to play in the State League, decided to head west with me. Life on the road was more appealing to them than playing in the League. They dug out their suitcases, too.

In Syracuse I had heard of James Tormey, a great basketball and football player from Georgetown University. I got in touch with him. Despite pressure from other teams, he agreed to swing west with the Globe Trotters. He had just finished his law school training. But before settling down into the routine of the courts, he wanted to give professional basketball a whirl.

Next I wrote Raymond Bradshaw of Schenectady who had played with my team in 1914 the year we won the "World Championship." Between Schenectady's entry in the State League and the Globe Trotters, he chose the Trotters. He dusted off his suitcase.

I needed two more. I received word that the famous Fond du Lac Company E was unable to organize a team that year. That meant a lot of basketball talent without jobs. One of these jobless stars, Pete LaPine, agreed to wear the Trotters' uniform. He would join the team in Chicago.

In the meantime I signed up Bill Schardt of Cleveland, against whom we played the year before. He could play with the team until February 5, when he would have to report for spring training with the Dodgers. LaPine would take his place. Finally Jerk Waters of Fort Plain agreed to go with us. That made the team. Or so I thought.

I made arrangements to gather the team together. Bradshaw and Waters were to meet Roberts and myself in Utica. From there we were to go to Syracuse where Tormey was to board the train. Then on to Rochester where we would pick up Johnny Murphy.

But Waters never showed up at Utica. Bradshaw and Roberts were discouraged, but I wasn't. I would have picked up a few conductors and trainmen to get a team if I'd had to.

Mike said to me, "Well, I'll go, but if Tormey don't get on at Syracuse, I'm coming right home again." Bradshaw nodded in agreement with him. . . . More worry for Basloe!

We arrived in Syracuse and there was no Tormey in sight. Roberts and Bradshaw took their baggage and got off the train. I was nervous but determined to stay on the train for Rochester no matter what happened.

Just as the train's whistle signaled to start, a tall man ran down the platform. It was Tormey. Back on the train for Basloe and Company. Roberts began to tell Tormey about Waters and Tormey said let's get off and not go, but I talked to him so fast the train started and we were off to Rochester to meet Murphy, the king of comedians.

Everybody was out with the "glad hand" that year. It always made the Western boys very happy to beat us. And all this interest made my pocket very happy, too. My team made an excellent record. Jim Tormey, the galloping attorney, proved he was a halfback as well as a basketball guard. He gave the Westerners the brand of play they liked best—slam-bang-head-on rough stuff. He drew a great many boos and hisses from the spectators, but it paid off. When the crowd did something Jim didn't like, he'd stop the game and lecture the people on their manners. They loved him for it.

Bill Schardt joined us for games through New York, Pennsylvania, and Ohio. Then he left us in Chicago. He was an excellent player, good off the backboards, a good shot, and a good gate attraction because of his baseball fame. Pete LaPine took his place.

We had more fun on this trip than we had ever had before. We drew packed houses, too. In Celina, Ohio, a small lumberjack town, they had a regular holiday, primping up for the coming of Basloe's world champions. Everybody bet on the home team except those slickers who couldn't make the town team of Celina. They were backing us heavily.

Well, Celina was bound to win. The referee, who was

dressed more appropriately for a funeral or a wedding than for a basketball game, was so excited coaching his team and taking advice from the wool-shirted audience that he forgot we were playing. So we had to call our own fouls. We just made it interesting so we could enjoy it. Tormey threw the Celina sports off his back so fast you would have thought he was rehearsing for an acrobatic act. Poor Mike Roberts was so banged up that when he laughed it hurt. He was bound to have the time of his life if it killed him. Celina won 21–17.

The crowd screeched for their new "Champions." I had left my championship banners at the hotel because I thought we would win. The Celina manager came across the floor to talk.

"Well," he said, extending a big mit to me, "I hope there's no hard feeling." After he squeezed my hand there wasn't any feeling at all. "You know," he continued, "you can't be champions forever."

I said, "That's right, boy, you're wrong again. You are not champions until I turn over the championship papers to you."

Then Mr. Manager wanted the papers.

I offered to sell them to him.

The fellow was very serious about the whole deal. I said $50. He went back across the floor to his players and began talking to them.

Finally he returned. All they could raise was $15. I was about to close the bargain when Mike and Bradshaw began to giggle. The manager got wise. We came near to having a young riot, but it all ended well. . . . Except that I didn't get the $15.

Since Fond du Lac had no team, I received an offer to represent them that year. All we had to do was wear their jerseys and play one home game a week. This was an opportunity that could not be overlooked. I rearranged my schedule to comply with the home game stipulation. We set off for Fond du Lac. Our opening game was January 26.

I decided that it would not be necessary to buy new uniforms. On the reverse side of our regular Globe Trotters jerseys I jut a big letter "E." If we played as the Globe Trotters, we wore one side out. If we played as the Company E team, we put the other side out.

Here's a letter written by Alden W. Thompson, Divisional Director of Wayne University, Detroit, on basketball in Fond du lac at this time:

As a kid in College in Wisconsin in 1914, '15 and '16, I played both with and against one or another of Basloe's teams. When I knew him, he called them the Oswego Giants, then later the Basloe Globe Trotters. The Co. E (Wisconsin National Guard) team of Fond du Lac was the top-notch professional basketball team of the Middlewest in those years, and Basloe would always include them and nearby Co. I of Neenah-Menasha in his itinerary. Numerous eastern teams came out that way, but he was a regular visitor and always with a great club.

In 1915 the Troy, N.Y., team came to Fond du Lac and played a three-game series with Co. E. I was invited by the Fond du Lac management to join their club for that series, which we proceeded to lose in a very efficient manner in three straight games, much to the dismay of the local fans. That Troy team was a great aggregation! It had many long-time greats on it—Inglis, Suils, Mueller, Haggerty, and Leary, besides both the Wachter brothers (one of them later a coach at Harvard). In those days a seven-man squad was an unusual expenditure of money that was hard to get. Players were expected to go the full game and the manager himself might suit-up just for the looks of things if he wasn't stationed at the door to count tickets. Parenthetically, I might call attention to the fact that the court at Fond du Lac was in keeping with the original use of the term "the cage game." It had a three-foot wooden fence all the way around the floor, emblazoned with local advertising, and a net from there to the ceiling. There was no out-of-bounds. You ducked through a gate in the fence onto the floor and the ball was in play all of the time. Both the players and the ball bounced off this fence, behind which the spectators sat on the main floor or behind the net on the balcony above on two sides and at one end and on the stage at the other end. Glass backboards are only now coming to be standard equipment, but the Fond du Lac court was equipped with them even in those days, though they were clear glass without the present day white outline or "target" markings. The Co. E team was one of the first, if not the first, in the Middlewest to have a complete roster of players on a monthly payroll, for playing basketball only, and it ruled that area from 1910 to 1916 in emphatic fashion, playing the best of the visiting teams and making an extended trip west each year.

When great basketball players are mentioned, there must be included the name of George Fogarty who captained and coached the Fondy team. Coming from the East originally, he was a great shot, an amazing dribbler, a fine floor strategist and, above all, a great competitor. He was the target for the top defensive tactics of every team he met, but he kept on scoring heavily regardless. I played against most of the men (then playing), and George Fogarty, for all around ability and knowledge of basketball, was the greatest of the lot. Walter Meanwell, Wisconsin U. and glamour coach of the Western Conference at that time, picked up much of his stuff from Fogarty.

In 1916 Basloe brought his Oswego Giants to Fond du Lac and then took over the management of that club, using two players from Fond du Lac. His team then wore white wool jerseys, with a big "E" on one side and a bigger "O" on the other. On the road he was Fond du Lac or Oswego as financial interest indicated. If Co. E was the drawing card locally, the jersey showed that big E, but if a New York team was a greater attraction, a simple twist of the garment gave that red O for Oswego its place in the night's sport picture. One of these jerseys was a prized and never-laundered memento of mine until some high school basketball player in Battle Creek "borrowed" it from me while I was coaching there.

We scheduled teams at Rockford, Ill.; Red Wing, Minneapolis, Chaska, and Bemidji, Minn.; Jamesville, Tomaha, Racine, Milwaukee, Green Bay, and Neenah-Menasha, Wis.—in fact, we scheduled so many teams right in Illinois, Iowa, Wisconsin, and Minnesota there was no need to go farther west.

We played eight games with Rockford, four in Fond du Lac and four at Rockford, before houses so packed that there wasn't even standing room. I recall a swell play that Mike Roberts pulled in one of the Rockford games. He was dribbling down the floor when a fellow in the audience knocked the ball out of his hands. Mike got so mad he kicked the ball right into the crowd. It hit a girl in the face and made such an impression on her that she was sweet on Mike for some time after.

The Rockford series was promoted by a most unusual sort of promoter. His name was Thomas Paputlis, a Greek restaurant owner in Rockford. He was a fat man with a fat man's million-dollar personality.

Tom used to say of basketball, "It's awful fast. I like it very much. Basketball players have very good eyes." Tom wore thick glasses.

I remember asking him if the style of ball we played was rough enough for him.

"Oh, yes," he answered, "just right. It suits me very much. I like to see lots of pushing and lots of knocking."

Some of Tom Paputlis' customers insisted he wasn't satisfied until he saw blood flow. I don't know about that. I think he liked basketball for the reason he told me—it wasn't dishonest like the wrestling back in old Athens. He appreciated honesty.

Thomas Paputlis had one suggestion to offer on how the game of basketball should be played. This was to make it absolutely fair for all players. He suggested that the baskets should be on a pulley attached to a rope. An official assigned to holding this rope should raise the basket when a tall man approached for a shot and then lower it an appropriate distance when a little man was about to shoot.

I asked him if he had any sons on the Rockford team. He sadly shook his head. He had only two nice girls, he said, but maybe some day basketball would present him with a good son-in-law. He liked American boys. "They are nice kids and like to work." Thomas Paputlis respected anyone who liked to work.

We got very friendly with the kindly Greek. He invited us to his restaurant for breakfast one morning. The meal was on him. Rockford had won the previous evening. We came a little late for breakfast, about 11:30; so we doubled up on the old boy and had dinner and breakfast combined. He was delighted.

It seems that Tom Paputlis got into the promotion game this way: The Rockford players couldn't find anyone to finance their efforts. One of Paputlis' daughters dated one of the basketball players. The daughter put pressure on Father. Papa agreed. Rockford had its team. "Pretty expensive," said Tom Paputlis. "Lots of fun and very easy way to get a headache." I agreed.

With his check for the guarantee in my pocket, I asked him to walk down to the bank with me so I could get it cashed. He was very anxious to go to the bank. He wanted me to meet the president. This was his way of impressing me with just how important a fellow he was in Rockford.

When we arrived, he introduced me. The president gave Tom a big build-up. Tom was Rockford's first citizen, a good businessman, a fine civic-minded sort, and so forth, the president said. Then Tom showed me how easy it was to get a little loan from the president, his pal. He left with $2000. It was for a few debts accumulated promoting basketball. Tom Paputlis made his X on the note. He could neither read nor write.

At Janesville, Wis., we played three games. They won two out of the three. And they would not come to Fond du Lac for a return match. At Red Wing, Minn., we split two games. Red Wing would not come to Fond du Lac, either. I made all sorts of boasts and threats in the newspapers to get these teams to play on our "home" court. But they wouldn't. I had many a running battle with loyal sports editors in these towns. In this way a great deal of interest was stimulated for the teams. People sided with one manager or the other. Threats were passed. The halls were packed.

About this time Clarence Johnson came on from the East to take Tormey's place. Johnson was a Colgate boy who had starred in college and State League play and who was now playing baseball with the Cleveland Indians. The team was even stronger with Clarence. The New York League managers were probably sore over my swiping players from them, but I could pay a bigger price and that's what the players wanted. I *was* the Federal League out West.

Poor Mike was like a lost dog without Tormey. He tried to break in on Murphy, but Murphy refused to chase around with Mike, who really went for the life on the road. He hoped every day would be a year.

I made Mike captain of the team, and he immediately began to crab with every referee on every foul called against us. He became known as the crab of all captains.

I was so flooded with offers of games that I finally organized two teams in Fond du Lac. Murphy had one team under the name of Oswego; Mike had the other under the name of Fond du Lac. No team in the country ever got the guarantees we got that year. I filled out the two teams with former Fond du Lac stars. On the "Oswego" team with Murphy were Fogarty, LaPine, John, and Morse. With the "Fondy" team and Mike were Young, Johnson, Bradshaw, Lilly, and Ziggy Thompson.

We were prospering indeed, receiving the largest guarantees paid in those days. Everyone wanted to play our "champions." Roberts and Murphy were being advertised as the highest-paid players in the United States.

In Red Wing that year we lost two games by the humiliating scores of 48 to 9 and 21 to 7. The headline in the local paper the next day read: "Red Wing Slaughters Fond du Lac Quint." They weren't far wrong. Ben Hawkins' team found us easy picking for two reasons. First, the game was played under amateur rules. Red Wing flatly refused to play the professional rules with which we were acquainted. As a result, we were like a swimmer in whirlpool rapids. Every move we made was a foul.

Added to the rule handicap was the floor. It was as slippery as an ice-skating pond. The Red Wing players wore resined shoes. They stayed upright while we fell down. It became a grotesque spectacle.

The second game was a real "basketbrawl." The referee might as well have stayed at home. Several times the crowd came out on the floor and attacked my team. During the second half Roberts and Hawkins both let fly with their fists. It was a good scrap, but Mike had a little shade on the big fellow and the battle ended in the first round.

After the first ten minutes, I had ordered my team to keep away from their men and not get hurt. I needed a team that could play the following night, also. Nevertheless the Red Wings continued to block and hold. Several times they slugged with closed fists. When Murphy would try to guard Hawkins under the basket, "Big Ben" would put that number sixty-two hand of his in Murphy's face and floor him. Yet the only foul the referee called on Red Wing was for kicking the ball.

Some 2500 fans witnessed the two struggles. I put up $500 for Red Wing to meet us on our home court in Fond du Lac, but they wouldn't accept the challenge. They insisted they were entitled to the World Championship banner. But I told them that this was not the custom because they must first meet and defeat us on our home floor in Fond du Lac. They said they could not come to Fond du Lac.

That was too bad, I said.

"Is that the only way we can win a World Championship banner?" they asked.

"Well," I said, "since you want one so badly, I'll tell you what I'm going to do. I'll sell you one for $50."

They bought the banner and were very satisfied with the deal. So was I. The same thing happened in Janesville. They beat us a game. Their manager, a live wire by the name of Caldow, couldn't understand why his team's victory didn't automatically entitle him to a World Championship banner. I tried to convince him the title could only be won on our home floor. He wasn't convinced. He wanted that piece of cloth.

"Tell you what I'm going to do," I said. "I'll . . ."

And I did. I asked $100 and got $50.

The Rockford manager also felt that, although his team had managed no better than an even break with us, they should get a banner. I made another $50. I would have done better except that George Fogarty was no believer in championship banners. He didn't hold them in proper respect.

We arrived back in Herkimer on April 19, 1916. The snow was almost gone. Farmers had begun spring plowing. Storekeepers were dusting off their roll-up awnings. The fresh smell from the river was good again. The season had been a huge success, and I had sold twelve World Championship banners. I gave each of my boys their double-duty jersey for a souvenir—the ones with the "E" on one side and the Oswego "O" on the other.

CHAPTER ELEVEN

"... AFTER THEY'VE SEEN PAREE"

WHEN the 1916–17 season came around, I needed the very best basketball talent I could get. Teams were forming in the West with stars aplenty in their lineups. Fond du Lac once again had a basketball organization. The publicity and success of the Globe Trotters had spurred other towns to go and do likewise.

But the West was not to put us in the shadow—not yet, at least. This season I discovered another great player in Leo Duval of Cohoes. He was a six feet, two-190-pound giant. Besides Leo, I signed Clarence Johnson again. I had my three regulars, Jim Murnane, Mike Roberts, and Johnny Murphy back. With this group wearing the Globe Trotter jerseys, I didn't foresee the need for more than ten World Championship banners.

We played 49 games in New York, Pennsylvania, Ohio, Indiana, and Illinois before reaching our old stamping grounds in Wisconsin. There we found that a new basketball power had arisen to challenge Fond du Lac for local championship rights.

When we arrived in Muscatine, we didn't expect the big stir that our coming had caused in the town. As the train pulled into the station at 1:00 A.M., we were met by a brass band playing by the light of flickering gas lamps, blaring their harsh greeting in the early morning air. The band marched us up the Main Street to our hotel.

The town was all excited about the coming series. Every seat in the hall where we were to play had been sold out in advance. The next morning I got up early and walked to the corner cigar store where tickets were on sale. I found that they had already taken in $900 for the game. We were guaranteed only $300. The local promoter had insisted the attendance would be small.

I went back to the hotel and called the Muscatine promoter-manager, George Volger. I asked him if he remembered that I was getting only $300 because he didn't expect a crowd.

He said, "Mr. Basloe, I myself am surprised."

They were charging $1.00 general admission and $1.50 for a reserved seat. So I said to him, "Look here, either we have $1200 guaranteed or we don't play."

This, of course, floored him. To ease the shock a little, I offered to include one of my World Championship banners. He couldn't refuse, not with the whole town expecting a game. So he agreed and we left for the bank. He put $1200 aside for me to collect at the end of the three-game series. Win, lose, or draw, I was sure of the $1200.

Back at the hotel, I found the boys lounging around. My roommate Johnny Murphy knew in a minute I'd been up to something. I was practically busting with the good news. So we laid out the World Championship banners to remove the wrinkles.

The Globe Trotters won the first game 18–16. Hundreds were turned away. The second game Muscatine won 20–16. But in this second contest, fans from surrounding towns like Dewitt and West Liberty were dissatisfied with the officials. They maintained that games as important as these should be handled by neutral referees. Local officials had done the job the first two nights, and the out-of-town customers thought too many Globe Trotters' goals were declared "no basket" and a foul called on the visitors instead.

When the teams came out on the floor the third night, the complaints of the crowd became so loud and strong that it was agreed the game would not be a championship contest. These fans had bets on the Globe Trotters.

Muscatine won the third game 19–18. The crowd betting on the Globe Trotters naturally didn't approve of the refereeing, and they made it very clear they didn't. There was a heated dispute at the end over which team had won. It came about like this:

During the closing minutes, Duval was in possession of the ball when he thought he heard the referee blow his whistle for the end of the game. Roberts had just made a basket to put our team ahead 18–17. Duval, for a lark, then threw the ball into Muscatine's basket. The referee ruled that the basket counted—against us. Muscatine was judged the winner. I protested long and loud. It didn't do any good. The referees stuck to their decision. The crowd booed and hissed, threatened and stormed. It didn't do any good. The decision stuck.

Anyway, everyone agreed that the Globe Trotters and Muscatine were just about the two best teams in the country. Muscatine had players like Bob Hasbrook, at the time the greatest center in the West; Abby Gould, fast and a great set shot (he pitched for the Cleveland Indians); E. E. Bloom, a fine all-around player at his guard position; and Healey and Lohr at the forwards.

Back in those early years of basketball when the sport was just "growing up," the idea of a team's selling a player was entirely new. It was rare even in baseball. But on this trip we had some trouble that forced me to sell a player.

Clarence Johnson was a swell fellow and a great basketball player, but he was touchy and quick-tempered. One day at Two Rivers, Wis., while we were waiting in the little station for our train to Manitowoc, the boys decided to play a little "five and ten." Jim Murnane grabbed his suitcase and put it on his lap for a table. Then we all huddled near the big round iron stove and began playing. Other people in the station crowded around. The cards were dealt. It wasn't long before the game began to get as hot as the stove. The boys kept raising one another until finally there was $12 in the pot and only two players left, Johnson and Murnane.

Now Jim was keenly observant of his opponent, and Johnson did not have the ideal poker face. So when Johnson said, "Four kings," Jim noticed a change of expression on Johnson's face. So Jim said, "four aces."

Wham! That was too much for quick-tempered Clarence. He grabbed the $12, dumped over the suitcase, flung open the door to the stove, and threw the money in.

All hell broke loose. We had all we could do to keep the boys apart.

After that it became apparent that if the team was to continue winning games and being a "team," I had to get rid of Johnson. With this in mind, I called Charles Wright, manager of Co. E in Fond du Lac.

"How much will you pay me for Johnson?" I asked.

"Why, Basloe, that's slavery," said Wright.

"You call it slavery; I call it business," I replied.

"How much do you want?" Wright wanted to know.

"Two hundred cash or $300 on time," I said.

"I'll give you $100 cash and pay you when I see you," he said.

"O.K. You bought Clarence Johnson for $100." And that was that.

I notified Johnson to report to Fond du Lac. He was pleased with the change. In fact, he wanted to settle down in the West. A few years after this deal, I learned that Johnson had died in an automobile accident in Minneapolis. He was one of the greatest athletes ever to graduate from Colgate. He may have been unmanageable when he lost his temper, but he fought hard and courageously in any game he ever played. Charles Wright never regretted the $100 he paid for Clarence Johnson.

We ran into a streak of bad weather. A blizzard stranded us in Beloit and caused us to miss a game in Janesville. Train schedules were snarled. One night we were due in the town of Two Rivers. We had to get the train from Appleton. There was only one train a day from Appleton to Two Rivers and that left at 12:30 P.M. We thought that would give us plenty of time to make the twenty-mile journey, but the station agent told us the train was a few minutes late.

"Let's play cards," said Murnane.

There was nothing else to do. We sat down and dealt. I hoped we wouldn't have another Johnson episode. We played from 12:30 until 4 o'clock. Still no train. Game time that night in Two Rivers was 9:00. But the station master kept insisting that the train would come. We were getting more and more uneasy. Finally about 4:30 we heard a toot down the track. Soon a train puffed in.

"Ha, ha," yelled the ticket agent. "Here comes a freight."

"But where's the passenger train?" I asked.

"Don't know," replied the agent. "You boys want to ride the freight?"

There was no choice. I had not purchased the tickets, and I thought I saw a chance to get a free ride. But as we walked up to the caboose, the freight conductor stepped out on his little platform and said, "Fares?"

"How much you going to charge to ride a freight?" I inquired.

"Ten dollars for the bunch," he answered.

Ten dollars was cheap enough. As I reached into my pocket to pay the man, Murnane stepped up, still holding the cards we'd been playing with in the station.

"Say, Bas, why don't you cut the cards with this conductor and see if you give him $15 or $5?"

The conductor was a gambling man; so we agreed. Murnane cut. I won. I paid the conductor his five and was about to climb up when Murnane stopped me. "Hey," said he, "how about five dollars for cutting the cards?" Great! I was bound to lose whether I won or lost. At least we kept the money in the family.

Riding a caboose wasn't so bad except that it took that blamed freight from 5 to 9:30 to go the twenty miles to Two Rivers. The local manager was almost beside himself with anxiety. He'd heard no word from us. He had a packed house waiting. People had fought their way through snow drifts to see this game. They would be ugly if we disappointed them. When he saw the freight come into the station instead of the passenger train he was expecting, he almost gave up.

But who should pile out of the caboose but the Basloe Globe Trotters. He was so happy he took us all down to a local restaurant and bought our supper (it wasn't in the contract). He sent word on ahead that the team had arrived but couldn't play until they'd eaten. That was all right with us. Riding cramped in a caboose for four hours didn't improve our muscles any. We needed time to limber up.

When the game finally started, it turned out to be one of the roughest contests we'd played. I don't know whether they wanted to beat us up because we came so late, or whether the manager wanted to get even for the lunch he bought us. Anyway it was rough. Roberts asked the manager, "Did you advertise a wrestling match or a basketball game?"

The wrestling got worse. Murphy got sore. He called time and left the game, telling me to take his place. In a few minutes he reappeared as an umpire, calling a foul a minute on the Two Rivers boys. The players kicked; the audience hissed; but Murphy kept on. By the second half everything was fine. We won the game, collected our money, and went out to have steak and onions.

We were in Plymouth, Wis., when we discovered that Mike Roberts was in love. He'd met a platinum blonde from Manitowoc, and had fallen for her head over heels. We had to agree that he had good taste, and we were all for notifying his folks so it wouldn't be such a shock if Mike should come home with a wife.

In the Plymouth game Mike got a little bruise. He kept complaining he was in bad shape and couldn't play. He asked me to send him back to Manitowoc for a rest. I knew he wouldn't get any rest in Manitowoc, but just to keep the kid in a good humor I let him go for the rest of the week.

Mike sought advice from Murphy and Murnane. These two had great sport with the young lover. Murphy told Mike that his papa and mama would be disappointed if this blonde couldn't make spaghetti with green peppers. Murnane let on as how he felt sorry for the bank roll Mike kept tied in a leather wallet around his belly.

In New London, Wis., we met a former Herkimer boy, Ralph Matthews. He was connected with the local Edison Club which sponsored the local team. But this time he wanted to see the locals defeated just to prove how good his hometown team was. We obliged, winning 27–22. After the game he was so proud of us that he gave us a party.

Being country boys, we were always ready and eager for any and all invitations, no matter from whom—that is to say if free eats were offered, we'd eat 'em. In Akron we got an invitation to have chow mein. A French lady who was staying at our hotel saw us play and invited the seven of us to eat with her in her suite. She was lonely, she said, because her husband was away on a buying trip. Besides, she insisted she liked country boys and admired us for our speed and strength.

I was so tired I wanted to go to sleep, especially since we were scheduled to play in Cleveland the next night. But the boys insisted. After all, they said, it wasn't often a French "dame" invited you to have chow mein in her suite. So I relented. We all went up together.

When we got to the suite, we found her on a bed with a green leatherette headboard. Either the hotel owner or her husband was in the dough. Maybe both. She already had a bad hangover by the time we arrived. She said the reason she had invited us to her rooms was that she got a great thrill out of watching our team play basketball. This was the first time she'd ever seen a basketball game. It was the first time we'd ever been invited to a French lady's suite.

We asked her, "Just what is it about basketball that you like?"

"Oh, the uniforms are so nice, cherrie," said she. "If ze girls want one of ze boys for a lovaire, before she say 'oui,' she know what she is getting."

The first French she taught us was "Oui, oui." It was always nice to say "Yes" in a lady's rooms, she said.

The waiter brought in the chicken chow mein and we all ate our fill. She asked us if the chow mein was good and we said, "Oui, oui."

When we had finished, she rang the little bell and the waiter came and took away the dishes. Then she invited us to sit on her bed. Mike Roberts, our dashing guard, sat next to the French lady. He asked her what the favorite sport was in France. She asked Mike to hold her hand while she told him. He did. Anything to make a lady happy. Especially if she wasn't feeling well. Then she undertook to explain to us what the real sport was in France.

"It is ze duelle," she lisped. "Fighting with ze pistole and ze rapier."

"But why do they want to fight with those things?" asked Mike.

"Why, ze just do," she said, somewhat confused with our obvious lack of education. "For example," she said, "suppose you (she pointed at Mike sitting next to her) should try to steal me from my husband."

"Not me," cried Mike, dropping the lady's hand and getting up from the bed.

"Oh, cherrie, it is just ze example," she said. Mike sat down again. "If you *did* steal me, my husband, he would get very mad. He would slap you with hees gloves. Then you would slap him back. Then you would meet somewhere with pistols. You would take your pistol and he would take his. You would stand back to back. Then you would march off fifty paces. Then you would turn and shoot at each othaire."

"You mean shoot at each other really?" asked Mike.

"But of course," smiled the lady.

"Then what?" asked Mike.

"That's all," she said. She made the motion with her finger of cutting her throat. "That's all."

"Some sport," said Mike. "Somebody's liable to get hurt."

"Oui, oui," she said.

"And your husband would do this?" asked Mike.

"Certainement. He is ze very brave Frenchman."

"That's all," said Mike, getting up from the bed and dropping the lady's hand again like it was a rattlesnake he'd been holding. We all got up and headed for the door.

"But where are you all going?" she cried, sitting up in her bed.

"Madame, we thank you for the supper," I said, "but we aren't so good with ze pistols."

"But you brave boys need not worry," she insisted.

"No thanks," said Mike.

"But the champagne, she has not yet arrived."

Neither had her husband and we decided to leave before he did.

Life on the road wasn't a bad life. My players never complained about the eats, or the beds, or the trains—much! But they enjoyed themselves just the same. Here's a letter Johnny Murphy wrote on February 3, 1917, describing the team's attitude toward globe trotting in general and a "Globe Trotter" in particular, Manager Basloe himself:

For the past four years Basloe has been writing (to the Utica *Daily Press*) letting you know the doings of the players, but he never mentions his own doings, so I thought I would let you in on a few.

Needless for me to tell you that he's "the champion hard boiled egg." We arrive in a town or city and hang around some street corner, while "Mose" sneaks around to all the hotels trying to get the best rate, and he positively refuses to go higher than 75¢ a night. Well, after about an hour of such shopping he finds the team on the same corner nearly frozen to death, and it's ten to one that the hotel he picks out is eight blocks away. But Joe always says it's just around the corner and we walk carrying two big grips. After locating in our rooms, he starts bumming razor blades, shaving soap, tooth paste, and cigarettes. After dolling himself up, he beats it out looking for a restaurant and then tells us what a swell steak he just had for 50¢.

On the way, he finds out where the tickets are on sale, learns the advance sale, and if it's a good one he calls on the manager and induces him to enlarge his guarantee.

The most fun the players have is to watch Bas get out of paying checks when he's in a party. It was funny last week in Sheboygan when a few Fond du Lac people attended the game and Bas suggested that they all go to a Chinese restaurant after the game and have a feed. Everyone agreed, and to make it all the better for Bas we all "egged" our way in for the "packs." Well, if a man ever sweated blood, he did that night. We all seated ourselves at the table, eleven of us, and everyone was looking at the menu, intending to order what he wanted. After looking at the prices, Bas turned to the waiter and said, "Charlie, bring in all Yokumian." We all dropped our menus and looked at Bas and saw that he was suffering. We could all tell that he was figuring out eleven times 15.

Well, you should have seen the look on poor Mose's face when Murnane ordered tea for the bunch, at 15¢ per pot. Roberts by this time had his appetite touched and asked for pie and seven others thought the same, but not Mose. He was satisfied with his 15¢ dish.

Down into his one-way pockets again for 35¢ when Murnane mentioned that it was pretty good pie for 10¢, and Bas looked sick. This was too much for him, and we realized that he was planning on how to duck the check because he started to laugh, but the laugh wasn't on the level. He got up, took a walk, looked at a phone book, railroad time tables, and did everything to stall for time, but we were wise and kept on ordering drinks till his bill amounted to $4.85, when Bas complained that he was getting sleepy and thought that he would go home, but suggested that the rest stay and enjoy themselves. But we all felt about the same and put on our coats and were at the door ahead of Bas.

He must have forgotten about paying because the cashier had to ask to whom does the check go? We all pointed to our manager and walked out. For once we stuck the manager.

The 1918–19 season got under way about a month after the first World War. The prospects of peace made sports and sports promoting look rosy. Western businessmen offered countless opportunities to me to come west with the Globe Trotters once again.

In less than three days I arranged over thirty games. I assembled a team and prepared for the journey. There was Jack Andre, a member of my team that handed the Buffalo Germans that famous defeat in 1910 after the Germans had won 110 straight. Since then, Jack had never been able to make another trip with the Globe Trotters because of the illness of his wife. At thirty, Jack was in excellent condition. I was very happy to have him on the platform at Utica the day we headed west.

Edward Kearney also was signed. He was but a young-ster of nineteen then playing with the Gloversville, N. Y., team. His speed, floor work, and shooting were to take the West by storm. The signing of this young man was a great piece of luck.

Blubs Alberding, a member of the 1913 and 1915 Globe Trotters, also made the trip, as did Jack Nolls. In 1916–17 Nolls had been hailed by sportswriters as the sensation of basketball. For a little man, Jack could outjump any center going.

This year's team had the prestige of former teams, but we did not travel the great distances the others did. So many teams had been organized in Ohio, Indiana, Illinois, and Wisconsin that we just never got any farther west. We played twenty games in Ohio alone and eighteen in In-diana.

In Columbus, Ohio, we met many friends who were proud to welcome Basloe's Globe Trotters for another sea-son. We defeated the local team 37–29. Jack Andre dis-played some of the finest open basket shooting that had ever been seen in Columbus.

John Lonis, a former Frankfort, N. Y., boy and a per-sonal friend of all the players from the good old Mohawk

Valley, had a drug store in Columbus, and he made it his business to see that the Globe Trotters from back home had a good time in Columbus. He and his friends arranged a reception for the team and he invited his friend Governor James M. Cox to the shindig to be held in the Elks Club hall. Lonis had played basketball back in the Valley with most of the boys on the Globe Trotters that year, and he had managed the Frankfort team when Jack Andre played on it.

When we arrived and were introduced to the Governor, we all tried to talk to him at once. He was very nice to us. He said we reminded him of a bunch of lobbyists. Mike Roberts wanted to know what a lobbyist stood for. Governor Cox tried to explain.

"My boy, they really don't stand for anything that I know of. They make a lot of noise in the capitol lobby, that's all." Mike didn't look satisfied, but he was afraid to ask more.

One nice thing about the dinner was we didn't have to worry over fancy table manners. It was good old-fashioned catch-as-catch-can. Everything was informal; everybody helped himself.

After the party that night we were all delighted with the hospitality of Columbus and the very gracious Governor of Ohio. We all thought it was too bad that a nice man like Mr. Cox was a Democrat. After the dinner, back at our hotel, the boys demanded the cost of a dinner from me. They were afraid I might consider the banquet as part of their allowance. Nobody put anything over on those boys.

Edward Kearney, the nineteen-year old wonder boy from Gloversville, couldn't quite get over the "World Championship banner" scheme. One day on our trip (no one had explained about the banners to him) he saw me unpack my satchel with the ten banners. I laid them out carefully on my bureau. Ed walked over.

"What are they?" he asked innocently.

"They are our World Championship banners," I replied.

Ed looked with awe at the pile of banners. "Did you win them all at one time?" he asked.

I looked at him in surprise. I'd thought everyone on the team knew about the World Championship banners. But not Ed. He was fresh out of high school. He believed championships were won and not bought. Well, I wasn't going to educate him. So I let him think we had won all the banners.

It wasn't long after that we lost a game in Ohio. As usual, following the game, I walked over to the manager of the opposing team and explained to him that now his team had become the World Champions. The manager was overjoyed.

"I suppose you want the banner," I said, looking as disconsolate as I could.

"What banner is that?" asked the manager.

"The World Champion's banner," I replied, trying to look surprised at his ignorance. "Of course you know about the World Championship banners, don't you?" I asked.

I then pulled out the banner from my bag and showed him. Ed Kearney came over about this time. He was horrified to see me offer the banner to the other team's manager.

"You mean we get this?" asked the delighted manger.

"Well, you won it," said I.

The manager extended his hand for the banner.

"Wait a minute," I cautioned him. "There's a small charge for the banner. It's $75."

The manager withdrew his hand. "Seventy-five dollars?" He went over to talk to his jubilant team.

Kearney looked at me with reproach. "You mean you've got to sell the Championship banner?"

"Yes, I'm afraid so," I replied. With $75 hanging in the balance, I didn't want Ed around; so I told him to go get dressed and I'd tend to the business. He left looking very sad to think that the team had lost and I now must sell the banner. All the time I was rubbing my hands with glee at the prospect of selling another piece of felt.

Soon the manager returned. He agreed to buy the banner, but all he could raise was $50. I agreed to let him have it for that.

Kearney played his heart out after that for fear we would have to sell another Championship.

On our way back that year, we again played the team that had purchased the banner Kearney saw. During the game, Kearney put in everything he had. As a result, we won by a handsome score. Kearney alone got 14 points.

When the manager who had bought the banner before was paying me the $150 guarantee, he handed me $100 in bills and the Championship banner in lieu of the remaining fifty.

Ed Kearney came over, proud as a puppy dog. "Mr. Basloe, I decided to bring that Championship back to the good old Globe Trotters, and I did."

What could I say? To young Kearney, championships were won, not bought. And to think I had to ask this kid's parents' consent before taking him out West! He spoiled almost every chance I had on that trip to sell the Championships. When I arrived home, I still had eight banners left out of ten.

In Kenton, Ohio, we had a great game with a record-breaking crowd. When the final whistle blew the score stood at 30–30. The mayor of Kenton asked us to play an over-time, to finish the game, but Jack Andre said, "Nah, we only agreed to play forty minutes."

Then the mayor got chummy. "Please, boys, go out and finish the game and I will do anything for you." Blubs Alberding came right back at the mayor and asked him to suspend the prohibition law and serve some real beer.

I stepped in at this point. A tie game and an extra game meant money for me. The mayor said, "Mr. Basloe, I am the mayor and dare not leave this court without finishing."

However, I decided it would be better business to play a return game. So I said, "We'll play your team Friday with a double guarantee and I'll throw in one of my banners for good measure."

The mayor was satisfied. The fans did a lot of squawking when it was announced that the tie game would go down in history. "To hell with history, play basketball," they yelled.

Altogether, an estimated 118,000 people saw us play that season. Grandpa Andre and young Kearney held up wonderfully well under the strain of life on the road, and the players received more money than any other players had ever received up to that time.

The 1919–20 season didn't start off very well. The team was entirely new that year. Murnane and Nolls became basketball promoters in the New York State League again and Johnny Murphy tried his luck at coaching in Rochester.

I rounded up Chuck Taylor of Columbus, Ohio; Bill Dowd; Jerk Waters of Fort Plain; Eddie Murphy of Ilion; and Carl Marriott of Herkimer.

The stamp of hunger was bitten deep into Chuck Taylor's face when he joined the team in Erie, Pa. He was a big, rangy kid with coarse-cut hair and a good pair of shoulders, but he looked too tired to play basketball.

The day he joined the team he had $15. The other boys got him in a pool game and won all his money. When I heard about it, I made them give it back to him, reminding them that I was the only hold-up man in the gang.

When it came time for dinner, he called me over and said he wanted his meal money in advance. I was surprised at the request. But I gave him the usual 35¢, and he left. I took the rest of the team with me for eats. Nobody on the team was very impressed with Chuck. They doubted he would fill his place on the team. But I wanted to give the kid a chance.

Pretty soon Chuck returned to the restaurant where we were eating. He had a chocolate bar and a glass of malted milk. From that day on, this was his diet. I didn't give a damn about his being thrifty, but I was concerned about how he was going to keep in top physical condition without any real food.

However, we hadn't played many games before I saw that Chuck Taylor was a great star. He never looked rested or well fed, but he certainly was saving money. I never knew what being on rations was until I met Chuck. It got so sometimes Chuck would shame the team when they used up their 35¢ or 50¢ for meals. By the time we got to Alpina, Mich., to play two games, Chuck had saved more money than all the rest of the team.

I had to leave the team for a few days to go to Detroit on business, and I put the team in charge of Bill Dowd. He was a great player, but a lousy manager. When I rejoined the team in Roger City, they were all broke. After the Alpina game they had met some players (not basketball) who were smarter than they were. Everyone on the team except Chuck Taylor lost money in that card game.

What were they to do? They had to get to Roger City. They all turned to Chuck, the boy who spent almost nothing for food and who saved every nickel he could. It was Chuck Taylor's money that got the team to Roger City. Of course, in the end it was Frank Basloe's money that repaid Chuck Taylor.

The new team was slow getting started. The boys weren't used to each other. We lost ten games or so before we hit our stride. After that, nothing could stop us.

When the 1920-21 season came around, I wasn't sure I would go on the road again. By then I had a family of two boys and two girls. My real estate and insurance adjusting business was growing fast. It required most of my time. In fact, I had just about made up my mind not to go again when Mike Roberts came to my office early in September. Mike told me about a team that he had coached up in the mining town of Harrisville, N. Y., the year before. Of the players he mentioned to me I knew only Bill Dowd, but according to Mike they were good and were already getting in shape for the season. Mike urged me to take them west. It was a hard decision to make, but the lure of the road was too much. Two months later, I had packed my bags, said good-by to my wife and kids, and started off on another Globe Trotting journey.

We started earlier that year than any year previous, leaving the last week in October. We played quite a few games in Central New York before going west, and by Dec. 1 we had behind us 26 games without a defeat. I was amazed at the prowess of this new team of Upstate lads. It was made up of Joseph Kellmurray; his brother, Shan; Donald "Toots" McBride; Mike Roberts—all of Utica; Bill Dowd of Frankfort; and Bill Ladeseur of Ogdensburg.

This team played more games than any other I had managed in the past and suffered fewer defeats. Our outstanding success was defeating Muscatine, Iowa, four times in a row. After this series, Beloit, Wis., challenged us to play a two-game series for the World's Championship. We agreed to play on the Muscatine court. After the two games, the team having the most points would be declared the winner. In 1920 these two, the Globe Trotters and the Beloit team, were the best in the country. Unfortunately, there wasn't an auditorium in the West that would hold the crowds who wanted to see this series. The hall in Muscatine would hold only 3000. We won the series.

While this series was going on, the New York Nationals team was making a swing through the West under the leadership of Garry Schemeik. They issued challenges to us in all the western papers. Finally we reluctantly accepted. We had everything to lose and nothing to gain from such a series. Fond du Lac was chosen as the site for the game. The winner would get 75 per cent of the gate and the loser the remainder. The game was played on Feb. 21. The new Fond du Lac Coliseum would hold 3500, and every seat was taken. We won 14 to 7.

It was in Muscatine on this trip that I came near to losing my good name. After we won the Muscatine series, the manager of the Muscatine Big Five, George Volger, and the players invited us to a cottage party on the bank of the Mississippi. The ground was covered with fine snow and the river was just beginning to freeze over with a thin coat of ice. Elmer Bloom had asked me to bring along a World Championship banner to show the boys. I obliged. As we entered, we first saw some one-armed bandits doing a big business. Lots of food was laid out on tables and everybody began helping himself. My team pitched right in. There were the usual introductions and drinks. But one glass of beer was all anyone on the team had.

As we made ourselves comfortable, three girls came out

with nothing much on and began dancing and mincing around, much to the enjoyment of the assembled crowd. I was a bit embarrassed and so were the kids. They were all quite young.

Suddenly the door at the rear of the room was kicked in and a voice shouted, "Stand where you are, this is the law!"

Everybody began running around trying to escape. Some men ran up to us and said, "Come on with us." They headed for a window, opened it, and jumped out—right into the ice-cold Mississippi. We decided we'd rather go to jail. The deputy sheriffs were running about herding together the panicky onlookers. "You're under arrest," they shouted. They emptied the one-armed bandits and told the girls to get dressed. But somebody had thrown their clothes into the river in the excitement and they couldn't oblige.

Nobody paid too much attention to us. "We haven't done anything," I told the boys. "They can't arrest us." We all decided to stay and see the thing through.

One of the deputies, Al Barry, called out to Frank Healy to get the judge. Soon a big fat man waddled in. Everybody called him Judge. His name was L. A. Crull. When some order had been restored, he said, "It's Sunday; so let's do the job here." I was wondering what would happen to our reputation if this incident should get into the papers. All the explaining in the world wouldn't get us out of this one.

The judge asked the sheriff to bring forward the first prisoner. They led "Toots" McBride before him.

"What's your name?" he asked.

"Donald McBride."

"Were you ever up before me?" asked the judge.

"I don't know," said Toots, "what time do you get up?"

Everybody began to laugh. In walked the four men who had jumped out the window into the river. All the onlookers crowded around us and began slapping us on the backs and laughing. Finally it was explained that the whole affair was a gag. The four men who had jumped out the window were acrobats hired for that purpose in the hope that we would follow them into the "drink." The "judge," the "sheriffs," and the girls were all part of the act. And so we stayed and enjoyed ourselves and took our good names home with us that night. I left a Championship banner for the cottage.

When the next season approached, I was even less inclined to take to the road than I had been the year before. My business was getting larger, my family was getting larger, and the sum of my years was getting larger.

But letters from managers in at least ten states combined to make a tempting proposition. I called in "Toots" McBride and Shan Kellmurray and discussed with them the possibility of another globe trotting expedition. We had made such a magnificent showing in 1920–21 that I was reluctant to let all this basketball money go to waste. There were many new teams out West eager to play us. The guarantees were much larger than in other years.

Some of my stalwarts were unavailable. Bill Dowd had signed to coaching at Beloit, Wis. Mike Roberts had signed up to coach at Muscatine, Iowa, and Bill Ladeaur had gone into the New York State League. Joe Kellmurray could not go. That left only McBride and Shan Kellmurray around which to build a team.

I thought at the beginning of this season that we would have a real struggle on our hands. But, as in most previous years, a "star was born." "Chubby" Goodman came from Middleville, N. Y. He was probably the first player to show the West the one-handed shot so popular today.

Bart Carroll of Massena, N. Y., a great football player with Colgate, also signed to go. But while on the tour, he received a telegram naming him football coach at Hamilton College. Bobby Shea, a youngster from Columbus, Ohio, just approaching nineteen, became one of our great stars. Then there was Jack McCoy, an excellent all-around player. In Rockford, Ill., McCoy received the sad news that his young daughter had died. He left for home and was replaced by Kenneth Eysaman.

I decided to undertake management of the team from my desk at home, with Shan Kellmurray as my road manager. We lost only 8 games out of the first 40 we played, and the games were all drawing excellent gates. Kellmurray was sending money orders home at the rate of three a week. When I saw this, I decided to join the team in Monroe, Wis., and help guide them for at least ten days.

Upon my arrival, I found that Goodman, our star, had a cold and a fever of 104 degrees, but was still playing basketball. They would place a pound of raw onions on his chest, gave him a pint of liquor, and we would be ready for all comers.

Financially, this was the most successful season yet.

The 1922–23 season, to be my last, came upon me faster than I expected, probably because I was getting a bit older. Early in the month of August, 1922, my mail was again filled with requests for games. To escape temptation, my wife and I went to Saratoga for the races. There we met three old cronies, Leo Duval, Butsy Collins, and Danny Laschen. Some perverse fate must have brought us together at the track that day. While we were reminiscing, along came Jerk Waters from Fort Plain.

Well, I just couldn't resist all that basketball talk. The upshot of the affair was the decision to make Trip No. 20— with the approval of my wife. Here were four excellent ball players with the assurance of good money in the New York State League, who nevertheless wanted the glamour of going on a 100-game journey out West. I couldn't refuse. Before the week was over, I signed up Charles Mallory, another star in the State League.

I appointed Mallory playing manager and Waters captain. When they were ready to leave, I packed twelve Championship banners in Mallory's bag. He wanted to know what they were for. Jerk Waters, acquainted with the workings of those famous banners, explained their use to the new road manager. By the time they arrived at Plymouth, Wis., where the outstanding team in that state was, they had won 49 and lost 6, but they had sold only three banners—and at ridiculous prices!

At Plymouth on February 4 they took a real trimming. Mallory telephoned the bad news to me. I got mad and took the first train for Manitowoc, Wis., where they were playing the next night. After becoming convinced that the boys had merely had an "off" night, and after watching them win at Manitowoc, I let the team go on by themselves while I made a trip to Plymouth to arrange another game, winner take all. We had to regain some of the prestige the team had lost. Besides, Plymouth had got a championship banner for nothing!

Manager Quinn refused to play us again. I offered to play his team at Sheboygan. He agreed if I would promote the games. This was more than satisfactory to me just so long as another game could be played between us to prove to the state of Wisconsin that Plymouth could be beaten. The contest was set for February 11.

The game drew a huge crowd. When the game was finished I had accomplished my purpose. We won 27–20. Dowd played guard for us instead of Glaschen. When we played near Beloit, he joined the team, provided he could get away from his duties as coach. Plymouth claimed they would have beaten us without Dowd.

In Rochester, Minnesota, we met the famous Mayo brothers and they showed us around their beautiful clinic. They had never seen a basketball game, but they promised us that they would come to see us play that night against the Rochester team. We defeated the Rochester team 32–20 and, sure enough, the Mayo brothers were there to congratulate us.

After a thirty-day swing through Minnesota, North Dakota, Wisconsin, Iowa, Illinois, and Indiana, we moved on to Detroit and a victory over the rarely beaten Rayls. Detroit was managed by Jerry J. Jackel, one of the cleverest promoters in the West. The coach was Ernie Wilson and the team had stars like Mike Maurer, pivot man from Michigan College, Dessert, Coveney, and Kennelley, forwards, and Marty Cavanaugh, guard.

The game was played in the Moose Hall and had a big ticket sale. Jackel arranged a cabaret show for the spectators after the game. The final score was 29–25. Both teams were in top condition, and they provided the fans with plenty of excitement. Mike Roberts and Bill Dowd both played with us that night.

Former Heavyweight Champ Jess Willard was at the game. Willard was a big bruiser. But he didn't look as though he wanted to hurt anyone. We found he was staying at the Cadillac Hotel, where we were. Back at the hotel after the game we found him and Johnny Coulon, former bantamweight champion, flirting with one of the hat check girls. Duval took a liking to her, too. Now this boy Duval was built like an ox. If he hit you, you were *hit*! Jerk Waters and Butsy Collins, a couple of kibitzers, started kidding Willard and Duval about the girl. They suggested they come upstairs and settle the matter in a little sparing match. The boys accepted and we all went up to my room.

Jess and Leo put on a three-round exhibition with Collins as announcer and Conlon as referee. It was an interesting performance, even though nobody got knocked down.

When the train pulled into Utica ending the trip, it also ended my career on the road. Looking through my papers at the end of this final journey, I found $5200 in promissory notes from some of the boys, collected during the twenty trips. Before I went to bed that night, I marked them all "Paid" and returned them to the signers. They had more than repaid me in the honest efforts and excellent services they rendered. I will never forget our fabulous journeys. Here is the won-and-lost record of my Globe Trotters-Oswego Indians:

	Won	*Lost*
1903–4	9	0
1904–5	16	0
1905–6	23	5
1906–7	26	3
1907–8	30	4
1908–9	38	2
1909–10	44	4
1910–11	54	3
1911–12	60	3
1912–13	86	10
1913–14	117	9
1914–15	121	6
1915–16	97	13
1916–17	111	13
1918–19	91	9
1919–20	94	16
1920–21	124	5
1921–22	89	17
1922–23	94	5
	1324	127

Miles Traveled — 94,800

I had proved to my father that I could make good. He always had harped on the idea that I never would. He had insisted I was wasting my time with basketball. It had been a very profitable "waste" of time.

In the fall of 1923 I made certain that there would not be another season of globe trotting. I became owner and manager of the Herkimer team in the New York State League. We played our games at Mohawk.

The opening game on Nov. 25 between Glens Falls and Mohawk is one I shall never forget. I arrived at the Armory in Mohawk about 6:30. One of the Glens Falls players was there ahead of the rest of the team. He asked me if I could play pitch. I said no, but I was willing to learn. The player said he would teach me. His name was Bucky Harris.

We went down to the card room where I was to get my first lesson in pitch. We were just about to start when a Western Union boy came in with a telegram for Bucky. He opened it and began to smile. He had just been made manager of the Washington American League baseball team for 1924.

Bucky was not only a great all-around basketball player, he was great at baseball, too. That next year he led Washington to the American League pennant and won the World Series.

In 1924 I became manager of the Mohawk Indians. I just couldn't keep my finger out of the basketball pie. But at least I was doing my baking at home now.

From 1923 to the Great Depression in 1929, I remained manager of the Mohawk Indians in the State League. During this time great changes took place in basketball. In the Spring of 1921 the two most famous teams in New York City arranged a series. The Whirlwinds and the Celtics, organized a few years before, agreed to play three games at the 69th Regiment Armory.

With the Whirlwinds that year were Barney Sedran, Marty Friedman, Nat Holman, Chris Leonard, Ray Kennedy, and Harry Riconda. On the Celtics were "Horse" Haggerty, Johnny Beckman, Whitty, Pete Barry, and Ernie Reich.

The Whirlwinds won the first game 40–27. The Celtics won the second game 26–24. Then the Furie brothers, managers of the Celtics, prevailed upon Holman and Leonard to leave the Whirlwinds and join the Celtics. This action brought some nasty comments at the time. It destroyed the Whirlwinds and made the Celtics one of the best teams in the nation. It also ended the series at two games.

This was the same year that the Friars of Beloit, Wis., and my Globe Trotters played their two-game series at Muscatine, Iowa, for the "Championship of the World." We won the series and then took on the Nationals of New York and defeated them also. I have always regretted that my great 1920–21 team never played the Celtics. It would have been a terrific match.

The Celtics went on to become the "big name" in basketball during the 20's and early 30's. They had the great advantage of playing out of New York City, a "big name" in itself.

In 1929 the State League broke up. It wasn't until 1934 that I again had a hand in basketball. Most of my time was spent at my real estate and adjusting business, but that year I brought the Rochester team to the Mohawk Armory for independent games with great teams of the East. Rochester continued to play their American League games at home.

About this time women began to figure in basketball in

many parts of the country. The greatest girl player of all time was the famous Babe Didrickson Zaharias. Her faking could tie opponents into knots. Her speed and dribbling were the equal of the best male stars, and she was an excellent shot.

In 1934 I arranged games for the "Babe" in Central New York. Her team won them all. She stayed at my home in Herkimer.

There were at least two outstanding girl teams, the Olsen Redheads and the New York Cover Girls. The Redheads had Hazel Walker for a star. The Cover Girls had Dot Whalen. These teams played male teams and rarely came off second-best. I doubt that such a thing as ladies in basketball was dreamed of in Lambert Will's time.

The American League had been organized in 1925 by John O'Brien. He's been president ever since. From time to time cities have joined and dropped out. The League was divided into two sections and playoffs at the end of a season decided the champions.

In 1937 the New York State League was reorganized in Syracuse. I became president. Cities included Buffalo, Syracuse, Binghamton, Elmira, Utica, Albany, Amsterdam, and Schenectady. With the war, the use of the armories throughout the state was denied the teams, and the League was forced to suspend operations.

When the 1947 basketball season came, basketball promoters with big ideas and big bankrolls met at Albany to try once again to form a state league. My younger son, Sheldon, attended this meeting. When he came home, he approached me with a big smile.

"Dad, you have been elected president of the famous New York State Basketball League," he said.

My wife was upset. Sheldon and I had to promise my

wife that we would have nothing to do with promoting the League—and basketball promises are very sacred.

The League had a meeting the following Sunday. I was escorted to the president's chair. Ben Danforth of Albany was made secretary and James Hughes of Albany became treasurer. In the League this time were Albany, Cohoes, Saratoga, Schenectady, Utica, Gloversville, and Mohawk.

I could see by listening to most of the owners there that day that they were strangers to basketball. I was sure they would learn a lesson they wouldn't forget.

We had $8000 in the treasury—$1000 from each member team. We had an excellent season as far as basketball was concerned. It was a players' paradise.

Sheldon's Mohawk team, the Redskins, made a great reputation, even though they finished second to Utica. They were invited to play at the World's Basketball Tournament in Chicago and also to play in Baltimore against the Bullets who had won the American League championship that year. Of course, this puffed Sheldon up mightily to think he had a team at the World Tournament the first year in the State League. His team made a great showing. But all this flattery cost me $3200. The rest of the promoters lost about $20,000. But they were not discouraged. They were sure the next year would be better, for they had learned a lot, they said.

In 1948 I was elected commissioner and Joe Thol of Albany became president. Glens Falls replaced Troy, and Albany and Gloversville withdrew. Oswego came in, but played only two months.

By the end of the 1948 season, Sheldon had lost $4100. Losses for the others again totaled around $20,000—this in spite of the fact that the basketball played was first-rate and all the teams were evenly matched. Cohoes and Mohawk played to capacity crowds, but their armories were too small to make enough money to pay their large over-heads.

But when the season ended, I had had enough. I re-signed as commissioner. Sheldon gave up coaching and managing because of poor health. Prominent businessmen of the Mohawk Valley, headed by Dr. James Gallo of Herkimer, took over the Redskins, but once more the owners lost money—this time about $5000. Not a club in the entire league showed a profit. In fact, losses amounted to nearly $30,000.

The League went through one more season, but when the treasury still showed a minus $10,000, it disbanded. In the American League, the only team that made money was Wilkes-Barre. In the B.A.A. League, Rochester and Minneapolis were the only clubs which made money. Pro-fessional basketball was losing money all over the country.

The Syracuse Nats of 1949–50, however, reminded me of the great teams of the past. They were a team without stars. All were great players and they had an excellent player-coach in Al Cervi.

Cervi was one of the first picked on the all-star team of 1948–49 in the National League. He came to basketball without a college diploma. He was a star with the Roches-ter Royals under the guidance of Les Harrison who also was a diploma-less star. In Syracuse they are finding out that with a man like Cervi and a team like the Nats basket-ball can again pay handsome dividends.

CHAPTER TWELVE

THE OLD GAME AND THE NEW

Now I think I'll swivel around in my chair and talk about basketball today as compared to basketball in my day.

The grand old cage game has come a long way from the football-like product of sixty years ago which you could see for 35¢ in the best country halls. (Of course, I can't understand why they still call it the cage game. It's no longer played in a cage. But more of that later.)

Sixty years' development of a game is bound to bring changes—some good, some bad. Perhaps the most obvious change in the style of play is the introduction of race-horse running from one end of the court to the other. This has led most fans to believe that present-day basketball is faster than the older product. As a matter of fact, I doubt that the claim is true. In the cage, for instance, I'm sure it was faster—as well as more scientific.

Today the sole object of the game is to get the ball down the floor and score, fast! Scoring is much easier today than it was in my day. Then a defense *was* a defense. We had elaborate plays for defending the goal. There was no ten-second rule. Play continued all over the court. The team with the ball passed it around as long as it wanted. When the team got ready to charge an opponent's defense, it did, and not until then.

Our quick razzle-dazzle type of ball handling would put to shame the so-called pass work on today's courts. In the old days the players did not depend on speed or height alone to overwhelm the other team. There was an exact skill to handling the ball. There are too many clumsy players in basketball today. Every coach or manager wants a seven-foot giant on his team. They believe that a man doesn't have to be fast, or shifty, or able to dribble or shoot, just so long as he can stand under the basket and drop the ball in from his chin!

The only modern team that uses the old razzle-dazzle type of play is the Harlem Globe Trotters of Chicago, and they are the biggest attraction in basketball. They don't run around like giraffes and awkwardly drop their baskets from the sky. Their superb footwork and ball handling has made them money and given them a national following.

This team was organized some twenty years ago. Their founder, A. M. Saperstein, was a fine athlete from Lake View High School in Chicago. Later on, when he was coaching at Wells Park, he became impressed with the showmanship and razzle-dazzle skill of colored players, and he decided to barnstorm with a select team of them. The name came easily. They needed something to indicate the team was a Negro unit. "Harlem" was a natural. They specialized in trick ball handling, a three-ring circus, vaudeville, and lightning basketball.

In 1940 the Harlem team won the National Pro Tournament in Chicago, and its subsequent successful tour of the country proved without any doubt that they played the brand of basketball the fans wanted to see.

Harlem's greatest victory came in 1949 when they defeated the Minneapolis Lakers in Chicago 61–59. They played to capacity crowds thereafter. In spite of their 1950 loss to the Lakers, they remained the most exciting team in the country to watch. They went to Europe and spread the gospel of good basketball there, becoming truly globe trotters. Typical of their won-loss record are these years: 1946–47, won 154, lost 3; 1947–48, won 152, lost 5; 1948–49, won 150, lost 6; and 1949–50, won 165, lost 9.

The Indianapolis Olmpians and the Harlem Globe Trotters are the bright hopes in professional basketball.

High-scoring has become the sole objective of the modern game, and in my opinion that factor has gone far toward robbing the game of its skill, speed, ball handling, and consequent excitement.

I shall probably be tarred and feathered for the following, but here's what I would like to see put back into basketball:

1. *The center jump after every point.* Back in 1894 the two smallest men on the team jumped center. There was no premium on bean poles. When the center jump was taken away in 1935 by the A.A.U., the pros soon followed suit. It removed the most spectacular play in basketball. All our plays in the old days used to start from center.

I know that just as soon as the center jump comes back, a great many fouls will be eliminated. Certainly something should be done to stop so much foul calling. The referees are whistle-happy. Of course, the referee is not to blame for this. The game has become so hysterical that the spectator now calls a foul before the referee sees it—providing it's against the other side's team. The game has been built up into such a relay race that contact is inevitable. Every little touch or brush is a foul. That's not the way basketball should be played at all. It is not a ladies' game. It is for men. In the early days referees used to get tired and sit down. At Albany the referee actually reclined in a rocking chair while the game progressed.

I remember back in 1919 in Janesville, Wis., when the Cardinals and my team played, there were only three fouls called in 40 minutes of play. We won the game 21–18. Nowadays, this would be fantastic. You couldn't play 40 seconds without three fouls!

With all these big, clumsy six-and-a-half-foot giants shuffling around the floor, it's no wonder so many fouls are called. There are a few exceptions, of course. George Mikan of the Minneapolis Lakers is an outstanding one. He plays like old pros used to play in my day. You can't get the ball away from big George, and he passes off, sets up plays, and hooks with either hand to perfection. He's master of the backboards and is so strong he can last a full game. He can fake like a smaller man; he knows the game perfectly and is always improving himself. He can stoop and pick up low bouncing balls like a normal-sized lad. And he's so big it's hard to get around him. He uses his elbows well and blocks out on defensive rebounds.

As an example of too much foul calling, take the Nov. 24, 1949, game between the Syracuse Nationals and the Anderson Packers of the National Basketball Association. The final score was Syracuse 125, Anderson 123. But what a time they had arriving at a final score! The game took four hours. Seven thousand people sighed with relief when it finally was over. There were five over-time periods played. But the most absurd feature of the game was the fact that 86 fouls were called on Anderson and 74 on Syracuse. Anderson made 57 fouls, Syracuse made 59. What a waste of time. Consider that a foul shot takes better than a minute. Then consider the 160 fouls called. Most of today's basketball is standstill basketball from the foul line.

2. *The cage game.* In the cage, the ball never goes out of bounds. It is always in play. The ten-second rule should be eliminated and the whole court should be used for the game once more. As basketball is played now, only half the court is needed. One-half is always empty. In my day, play was all over. This was possible because the courts were much shorter. They should be shorter now, too. The shorter court calls for a different type of defense. In the game of thirty years ago it was necessary to keep a defensive man in the backcourt at all times. The greatest defending guards were Andy Suils of Troy and Johnny Murphy of the Globe Trotters.

Of course, our guards knew how to shoot accurately. There wasn't a better shot under the basket than Mike Roberts or a better shot at a short angle than Jim Murnane. Yet guards in those days had to be more rugged than forwards because they had to defend against the hardest and fastest chargers on the opponent's team.

Defense then was like modern ice hockey defense, with guards blocking out the fast-moving forwards. The fans loved the contact. But as the game "progressed," another type of basketball crept in. Guards were moved up into scoring position. This meant the defense was weaker. Basketball became a contest in which each team tried to score the most points in 40 minutes.

3. *Open baskets.* Since fans like big scores, I don't suppose that the open basket will ever come back. It took skill to score in one of these. Without a backboard, the shooter had to hit the basket or he failed to score. And there was none of this re-bound stuff. Most of today's baskets are scored by the bean pole under the basket tipping the ball in after another player farther out has missed his shot. With the backboard and the tall man, all the beautiful passing, dribbling, and set-plays have been thrown out the

window. They had better open the window and throw them back in again for the good of the game.

4. *Smaller squads.* In my day, we traveled with six men and played all our games without substitutions. If someone was hurt so badly he couldn't dress, I would take his place. One time we used local talent. But my boys had pluck. They could play 40 minutes of sport without dropping in a heap. Ask a modern player to do that and he'll tear up his contract and go elsewhere. Remember Chubby Goodman playing in Wisconsin with a fever of 104 degrees? That wasn't unusual. Jim Murnane once played with two cracked ribs.

Not that I want to see anyone today play with a fever or with some unmended vertabrae. But the long line of substitutes warming the benches today means a slower game, one with less skill and pluck. That's one thing the Globe Trotters had plenty of—pluck. Because of the five-foul limit now and the number of fouls called, they have to have big squads just to last 40 minutes! We didn't have this problem.

Today a player can become a hero in a matter of seconds. Have you never seen a game in which a man goes in and scores the winning point in the final seconds? Likewise in baseball there are one-pitch heroes; in football there are one-pass heroes. But in the old days, you played the whole game and earned your hero rating if you could. If you scored the winning point in the last few seconds, you had something to be proud of. You had earned your reward. The tight-defense style of play made it much harder to be a one-minute hero. Few scores were racked up in a minute's time.

There's at least one respect in which modern basketball is better than horse-and-buggy basketball. In my day, home refereeing was the rule. Many times in games on the road we ran into obvious favoritism from officials. Today's referees, although too fond of their whistles, usually try to be impartial. The fans are a little more charitable toward that sometimes unhappy breed of men, too.

I remember a story that Chuck Meehan told of his refereeing experience in Troy, N.Y. As he was walking into the armory the night of the game with his bag in his hand, a little kid ran up to him and said, "Carry your bag, mister?"

You see, the boy wanted to get into the game for nothing, which he could do by carrying one of the players' bags. Chuck handed the kid his bag and continued up the steps of the armory.

"Playing for Troy, mister?" the kid asked. Chuck said he wasn't. The kid then asked if he was playing for the visitors. Chuck said he wasn't playing for the visitors either.

With that the kid put Chuck's bag down and started to back away. "I know," he said with as near a sneer as he could muster, "you're the referee. Well, mister, I'll tell you this before you start. You stink!"

One time in Amsterdam they had to keep both teams and the referee locked in the cage between the halves so the crowd couldn't get at them. When the game was over, good-hearted citizens formed an alley through which they could run to the dressing room. Then, when everyone had dressed, they had to wait until the last minute to get the train out of town because they got word the fans were waiting for them with rocks at the railroad station.

It wasn't unusual for fans to throw cigarettes at the players. Sometimes chairs came hurtling out. Once a lady stuck her hatpin into one of my players as he came charging down the floor. Many times out West the crowds would come out onto the floor spoiling for a fight. It took fast talking to stop riots sometimes. There was the experience in Fond du Lac when I had to call out the militia to escort us from the floor. Such was basketball in the old days.

Basketball has changed far more radically since its inception than have America's other two major sports, baseball and football. It has been mauled, twisted, and turned topsy-turvy to such an extent that I can hardly recognize the game I have played, promoted, and watched since childhood. I only wish that those enthusiasts who believe it is a better game today than it used to be could have seen one of our games played, say, in 1915.